The Codependency Cure

Self-help, Volume 9

Timothy Scott Phillips

Published by Arcane Horizons Publishing, 2024.

While every precaution has been taken in the preparation of this book, the publisher assumes no responsibility for errors or omissions, or for damages resulting from the use of the information contained herein.

THE CODEPENDENCY CURE

First edition. December 3, 2024.

Copyright © 2024 Timothy Scott Phillips.

ISBN: 979-8230430537

Written by Timothy Scott Phillips.

Table of Contents

To those who have felt lost in the shadows of others,

May you find the courage to rediscover yourself, the strength to set boundaries,

and the wisdom to build relationships rooted in mutual respect and love.

This book is for you—your journey to healing begins here.

Chapter 1: Understanding Codependency

Definition and Characteristics of Codependency

Codependency is a complex and often misunderstood concept, but at its core, it refers to a behavioral condition in a relationship where one person enables another person's addiction, poor mental health, immaturity, irresponsibility, or underachievement. The term was originally coined in the context of Alcoholics Anonymous to describe the behavior patterns of family members of alcoholics. However, over time, it has come to encompass a broader range of dysfunctional relationship dynamics.

A key characteristic of codependency is an excessive reliance on other people for approval and a sense of identity. People who struggle with codependency often have low self-esteem and may seek validation through their relationships, putting the needs of others before their own to an unhealthy extent. They might have difficulty setting boundaries, leading to an over-involvement in the lives of others.

Characteristics of Codependency

1. EXCESSIVE CARETAKING: Codependent individuals often go to great lengths to care for others, even at their own expense. They might feel responsible for other people's happiness and well-being, neglecting their own needs in the process.

2. People-Pleasing: A strong desire to be liked and accepted can drive codependent behavior. Individuals may find it hard to say no and often agree to things they do not want to do to avoid conflict or rejection.

3. Control Issues: Despite often appearing passive, codependent individuals may exert a great deal of control over others to feel safe and secure. This control can manifest through manipulation, guilt-tripping, or other indirect means.

4. Poor Boundaries: Boundaries are essential for healthy relationships, but codependent individuals often struggle with them. They might have blurred or non-existent boundaries, making it hard to separate their own needs and feelings from those of others.

5. Low Self-Esteem: Many people who struggle with codependency have a poor self-image. They may feel unworthy or unlovable, driving them to seek validation through their relationships.

6. Denial: Codependency often involves a significant amount of denial. Individuals might downplay or ignore their own emotional pain and problems, focusing instead on others.

7. Dependency: Codependent individuals may rely heavily on others for their sense of self-worth and identity. This dependency can make it difficult for them to function independently.

History and Origins of the Concept

THE CONCEPT OF CODEPENDENCY emerged from the field of addiction and recovery. In the 1950s, as Alcoholics Anonymous (AA) and other recovery programs began to gain prominence, professionals noticed that family members of alcoholics exhibited specific behavioral patterns. These patterns often involved enabling behaviors, where family members would inadvertently support the alcoholic's addiction.

The term "codependency" itself began to gain traction in the 1980s, largely due to the work of therapists and counselors who specialized in addiction. Melody Beattie's book "Codependent No More," published in 1986, played a significant role in popularizing the term and concept. Beattie, who was herself a recovering addict, described codependency as a pattern of behavior where individuals allowed the behavior of another to affect them and were obsessed with controlling that behavior.

Early research and literature on codependency focused heavily on its connection to addiction. However, as the concept evolved, it became clear that codependency could occur in a wide range of dysfunctional relationships, not just those involving substance abuse. Today, codependency is recognized as a broader relational pattern that can exist in various contexts, including relationships with family members, friends, and romantic partners.

Common Misconceptions About Codependency

DESPITE ITS RECOGNITION in the fields of psychology and counseling, codependency remains a somewhat controversial and often misunderstood concept. Several misconceptions persist, which can hinder understanding and effective intervention.

Misconception 1: Codependency Only Occurs in Relationships with Addicts

WHILE CODEPENDENCY was first identified in the context of relationships with addicts, it is not limited to these situations. Codependent behaviors can emerge in any relationship where there is an imbalance of power and a pattern of enabling unhealthy behavior. This can include relationships with individuals who have mental health issues, chronic illness, or even those who are simply emotionally immature or irresponsible.

Misconception 2: Codependent Individuals are Just Being "Nice"

IT'S EASY TO MISTAKE codependent behavior for simple kindness or care. However, there is a significant difference between healthy caregiving and codependency. In healthy relationships, caregiving is mutual and balanced, whereas in codependent relationships, one person often sacrifices their own needs and well-being to take care of another, leading to an unhealthy dynamic.

Misconception 3: Codependency is the Same as Dependency

WHILE THE TWO TERMS sound similar, codependency and dependency are not the same. Dependency refers to a reliance on someone else for support and care, which can be a normal part of healthy relationships. Codependency, on the other hand, involves an unhealthy level of dependence where one's sense of self-worth and identity is tied to the relationship, often leading to controlling behaviors and poor boundaries.

Misconception 4: Only Women are Codependent

CODEPENDENCY IS OFTEN stereotyped as a predominantly female issue, partly due to cultural norms around caregiving and nurturing. However, men can and do experience codependency. The patterns may manifest differently due to societal expectations, but the underlying dynamics of codependency do not discriminate based on gender.

Misconception 5: Codependency is a Permanent Condition

WHILE CODEPENDENCY can be deeply ingrained, it is not a permanent condition. With awareness, therapy, and effort, individuals can learn to develop healthier relationship patterns. Recovery involves learning to set boundaries, build self-esteem, and develop a stronger sense of self-worth independent of others.

Misconception 6: Codependency is Always Bad

NOT ALL ASPECTS OF codependency are inherently negative. The traits associated with codependency, such as empathy, loyalty, and a strong desire to care for others, can be positive when expressed in healthy ways. The goal is not to eliminate these traits but to learn to express them in a balanced and healthy manner.

The Broader Context of Codependency

TO FULLY UNDERSTAND codependency, it is important to consider it within the broader context of human relationships and societal influences. Our culture often glorifies self-sacrifice and caregiving, especially among women, which can inadvertently promote codependent behaviors. Additionally, certain family dynamics, such as enmeshment or overprotectiveness, can contribute to the development of codependent patterns.

Codependency also intersects with other psychological concepts and conditions. For example, individuals with codependent tendencies may also struggle with anxiety, depression, or personality disorders. Understanding these intersections can provide a more comprehensive view of the condition and inform more effective treatment approaches.

Moving Forward

UNDERSTANDING CODEPENDENCY is the first step towards addressing and overcoming it. By recognizing the characteristics and origins of codependency, individuals can begin to identify these patterns in their own lives. The journey to recovery involves developing healthier relationship dynamics, building self-esteem, and learning to set boundaries. While the path may be challenging, it is possible to break free from codependent patterns and build relationships that are balanced, fulfilling, and healthy.

In the following chapters, we will explore these topics in greater detail, providing practical strategies and tools to help individuals on their journey towards healing and healthy relationships. The goal is to empower readers with the knowledge and skills they need to create a life that is not defined by codependency but by mutual respect, self-worth, and genuine connection.

Chapter 2: Recognizing the Signs

Codependency can be elusive and difficult to identify, especially for those who are living it. Understanding the emotional, behavioral, and psychological symptoms is crucial in recognizing codependency. This chapter will delve into these symptoms, provide case studies and real-life examples to illustrate them, and offer self-assessment quizzes and tools to help you identify codependent tendencies in yourself or others.

Emotional Symptoms of Codependency

EMOTIONAL SYMPTOMS of codependency often revolve around low self-esteem, anxiety, and a deep sense of responsibility for others' feelings and behaviors. These symptoms can manifest in various ways:

1. Low Self-Esteem: Codependent individuals often struggle with feelings of inadequacy and self-doubt. They may believe they are unworthy of love and respect unless they are making significant sacrifices for others.

2. Anxiety and Worry: There is a constant state of anxiety about the well-being of others. Codependent individuals often feel nervous and worried when others are unhappy or in distress, feeling compelled to fix their problems.

3. Guilt and Shame: Feeling guilty for other people's problems or emotions is common. Codependents may also experience shame about their own needs and emotions, believing that they are selfish for prioritizing themselves.

4. Emotional Numbness: To cope with overwhelming emotions, codependent individuals may detach and become emotionally numb. They might have difficulty identifying and expressing their own feelings.

5. Resentment: Despite their self-sacrificing behavior, codependent individuals often feel resentment towards others for not reciprocating or appreciating their efforts. This can lead to feelings of anger and bitterness.

6. Fear of Abandonment: A deep-seated fear of being abandoned or rejected drives many codependent behaviors. This fear can lead to clinging to unhealthy relationships and avoiding conflict at all costs.

Behavioral Symptoms of Codependency

BEHAVIORAL SYMPTOMS of codependency are characterized by actions that seek to control, fix, or overly care for others, often at the expense of one's own well-being. Key behavioral symptoms include:

1. Over-Caretaking: Codependent individuals often take on the role of caregiver, going to great lengths to meet the needs of others. This can include making significant personal sacrifices, such as time, money, and emotional energy.

2. People-Pleasing: There is a strong desire to please others, often leading to saying yes to requests and demands even when it is inconvenient or detrimental to oneself. Codependents may avoid expressing their own needs and desires.

3. Difficulty Setting Boundaries: Codependent individuals struggle to establish and maintain healthy boundaries. They may allow others to infringe on their personal space, time, and resources without objection.

4. Enabling: In an attempt to help, codependents may enable unhealthy behaviors in others, such as substance abuse, irresponsibility, or emotional dependence. This behavior perpetuates the cycle of dysfunction.

5. Control Issues: Despite a seemingly passive demeanor, codependent individuals often try to control others' behaviors and emotions. This control can be subtle, such as manipulation through guilt or more overt efforts to manage others' lives.

6. Neglecting Self-Care: The focus on others' needs often leads to neglecting one's own self-care. This can include poor physical health, lack of personal hobbies and interests, and ignoring one's emotional and mental well-being.

7. Sacrificing Personal Goals: Codependents may abandon their own goals and aspirations to support or accommodate others. This can result in a loss of personal identity and fulfillment.

Psychological Symptoms of Codependency

PSYCHOLOGICAL SYMPTOMS of codependency often involve cognitive distortions and unhealthy thought patterns that reinforce codependent behaviors. These include:

1. Black-and-White Thinking: Codependents often see situations in extremes. They may view themselves as entirely responsible for others' problems or believe that their efforts are the only thing keeping others afloat.

2. Catastrophizing: There is a tendency to expect the worst possible outcome in any situation, leading to heightened anxiety and overreaction to perceived threats or problems.

3. Mind Reading: Codependent individuals may assume they know what others are thinking or feeling, often believing they are the cause of others' negative emotions. This leads to unnecessary guilt and worry.

4. External Locus of Control: Codependents often believe that their happiness and well-being depend entirely on external factors, such as the approval and behavior of others, rather than internal self-worth and autonomy.

5. Over-Responsibility: There is a pervasive belief that they are responsible for others' happiness and success. This can lead to taking on excessive responsibilities and feeling overwhelmed.

Case Studies and Real-Life Examples

TO BETTER ILLUSTRATE these symptoms, let's look at a few case studies and real-life examples.

Case Study 1: Sarah and Her Husband John

SARAH IS A 45-YEAR-old woman who has been married to John for 20 years. John has struggled with alcohol addiction for most of their marriage. Sarah's codependency manifests in her constant efforts to manage John's drinking. She hides his alcohol, makes excuses for his behavior, and takes on the responsibility of maintaining their household and finances.

Emotionally, Sarah experiences low self-esteem and believes that her worth is tied to her ability to keep John sober. She is constantly anxious about his drinking and feels guilty when he relapses. Despite feeling resentful and exhausted, Sarah is afraid of leaving John because she fears being alone and believes she is responsible for his well-being.

Behaviorally, Sarah's over-caretaking and enabling are evident. She neglects her own needs and interests, focusing entirely on John's recovery. Her difficulty in setting boundaries allows John to continue his destructive behavior without facing the consequences.

Psychologically, Sarah engages in black-and-white thinking, believing that she is the only one who can save John from his addiction. She catastrophizes about the future, fearing that if she stops helping him, their lives will fall apart.

Case Study 2: Mark and His Mother Linda

MARK IS A 30-YEAR-OLD man who lives with his mother, Linda. Linda has chronic health issues and relies heavily on Mark for support. Mark's codependency is evident in his over-involvement in his mother's life. He manages her medications, attends all her doctor's appointments, and has put his own career on hold to take care of her.

Emotionally, Mark feels a deep sense of guilt and responsibility for his mother's well-being. He experiences anxiety whenever he considers pursuing his own goals and dreams, fearing that his mother will suffer without his constant attention. Mark struggles with low self-esteem, believing that his worth is tied to his role as a caregiver.

Behaviorally, Mark's people-pleasing and difficulty setting boundaries are apparent. He rarely says no to his mother's requests, even when they are unreasonable. He neglects his social life and personal interests to be available for her at all times.

Psychologically, Mark engages in mind reading, assuming that his mother will be unhappy or disappointed if he prioritizes his own needs. He has an external locus of control, believing that his happiness is dependent on his mother's approval and well-being.

Real-Life Example: Emily and Her Friend Laura

EMILY IS A 28-YEAR-old woman with a close friend, Laura, who has a pattern of unstable relationships and emotional crises. Emily's codependency is evident in her constant efforts to rescue Laura from her problems. She offers emotional support, financial assistance, and often drops everything to be there for Laura whenever she calls.

Emotionally, Emily feels responsible for Laura's happiness and experiences anxiety whenever Laura is upset. She struggles with guilt, believing she is not doing enough to help her friend. Emily's low self-esteem leads her to seek validation through her role as Laura's savior.

Behaviorally, Emily's over-caretaking and enabling are clear. She neglects her own needs and responsibilities, focusing on Laura's crises. Her difficulty setting boundaries allows Laura to become increasingly dependent on her support.

Psychologically, Emily engages in over-responsibility, believing that she is the only one who can help Laura navigate her problems. She catastrophizes about Laura's future, fearing that without her constant support, Laura's life will fall apart.

Self-Assessment Quizzes and Tools

RECOGNIZING CODEPENDENCY in oneself or others can be challenging. The following self-assessment quizzes and tools can help identify codependent tendencies. These assessments are not diagnostic tools but can provide insight into patterns of behavior and thought that may indicate codependency.

Self-Assessment Quiz: Am I Codependent?

ANSWER THE FOLLOWING questions honestly. For each statement, rate how often it applies to you on a scale of 1 to 5, with 1 being "Never" and 5 being "Always."

1. I feel responsible for solving other people's problems.

2. I prioritize others' needs over my own.

3. I feel guilty when I say no or set boundaries.

4. I seek approval and validation from others.

5. I have difficulty identifying and expressing my own feelings.

6. I feel anxious when others are upset or unhappy.

7. I neglect my own self-care to take care of others.

8. I struggle with low self-esteem and self-worth.

9. I feel resentful when others do not appreciate my efforts.

10. I fear being abandoned or rejected.

Scoring:

- 10-20: Low likelihood of codependency.

- 21-30: Moderate likelihood of codependency.

- 31-40: High likelihood of codependency.

- 41-50: Very high likelihood of codependency.

Boundary Setting Exercise

SETTING BOUNDARIES is crucial in overcoming codependency. Use the following exercise to practice identifying and setting healthy boundaries.

1. Identify an area in your life where you feel your boundaries are being violated. This could be a relationship, work situation, or social commitment.

2. Reflect on how this boundary violation affects your emotional and mental well-being. Write down your thoughts and feelings.

3. Consider what a healthy boundary would look like in this situation. What do you need to feel respected and valued?

4. Plan how you will communicate this boundary to the relevant person or people. Be clear and assertive in your communication, using "I" statements to express your needs.

5. Practice enforcing this boundary. Be prepared for resistance and remain firm in your commitment to your well-being.

Journaling Prompts for Self-Reflection

JOURNALING CAN BE A powerful tool for self-reflection and insight. Use the following prompts to explore your thoughts and feelings related to codependency.

1. What are my earliest memories of feeling responsible for others' emotions or problems?

2. How do I feel when I prioritize my own needs and desires? What thoughts and emotions arise?

3. In what ways do I seek validation from others? How does this affect my self-esteem?

4. What are my fears around setting boundaries and saying no? How can I address these fears?

5. How do I define my sense of self-worth? What steps can I take to build a stronger sense of self?

Support System Inventory

HAVING A SUPPORT SYSTEM is essential in overcoming codependency. Use the following inventory to assess your current support system and identify areas for improvement.

1. List the people in your life who provide emotional support. How often do you rely on them for validation and reassurance?

2. Identify any relationships where you feel your boundaries are being violated. How can you address these boundary issues?

3. Consider whether you have any relationships that are primarily one-sided. How can you create more balanced, reciprocal relationships?

4. Reflect on your involvement in support groups, therapy, or other resources for personal growth. How can you increase your engagement in these areas?

5. Plan how you will build a stronger support system. This might include seeking therapy, joining a support group, or cultivating new friendships.

Conclusion

Recognizing the signs of codependency is a crucial step in the journey towards recovery. By understanding the emotional, behavioral, and psychological symptoms, examining real-life examples, and utilizing self-assessment quizzes and tools, individuals can gain insight into their own patterns and begin to take action towards healthier relationships and self-worth.

In the following chapters, we will explore strategies for breaking codependent patterns, building self-esteem, and developing healthy relationships. The path to recovery is challenging but achievable, and with the right knowledge and support, it is possible to overcome codependency and create a fulfilling, balanced life.

Chapter 3: The Roots of Codependency

———

Understanding the roots of codependency is crucial for those looking to overcome it. Codependency often originates in early family dynamics and childhood experiences, is reinforced by trauma and past relationships, and is shaped by societal and cultural factors. This chapter explores these foundational aspects to provide a comprehensive view of how codependent behaviors develop and persist.

Family Dynamics and Childhood Experiences

THE FAMILY ENVIRONMENT is where individuals first learn about relationships, communication, and self-worth. Dysfunctional family dynamics can significantly contribute to the development of codependency. Several key factors in family dynamics and childhood experiences play a role:

1. Parentification

PARENTIFICATION OCCURS when a child is forced to take on the role of a caregiver to their siblings or even their parents. This can happen in families where parents are absent, addicted, or otherwise unable to fulfill their parental roles. The child learns to prioritize the needs of others over their own, setting the stage for codependent behaviors in adulthood.

Example: A young girl named Jane grew up in a household where her mother struggled with alcoholism. Jane often had to care for her younger siblings, cook meals, and handle household chores. As an adult, Jane finds herself unable to focus on her own needs and constantly feels responsible for the well-being of others.

2. Enmeshment

ENMESHMENT DESCRIBES a lack of boundaries between family members, where individuals are overly involved in each other's lives. This can lead to difficulties in establishing personal boundaries and a strong sense of responsibility for others' emotions and behaviors.

Example: Tom grew up in a family where his parents were overly involved in his life, making decisions for him and expecting him to share all his thoughts and feelings with them. As an adult, Tom struggles to set boundaries in his relationships and feels guilty when he tries to assert his independence.

3. Neglect and Emotional Unavailability

CHILDREN WHO GROW UP in neglectful environments or with emotionally unavailable parents may develop codependent behaviors as a means of seeking validation and affection. These children often learn that their needs are unimportant and that they must earn love and attention by taking care of others.

Example: Maria's parents were emotionally distant and rarely expressed affection or interest in her life. In her adult relationships, Maria goes out of her way to please others, hoping to earn the love and attention she craved as a child.

4. Role Reversal

IN SOME FAMILIES, CHILDREN are placed in a position where they are expected to meet the emotional needs of their parents. This role reversal can lead to feelings of inadequacy and a constant drive to prove their worth through caretaking.

Example: Kevin's mother relied on him for emotional support, often confiding in him about her marital problems and personal struggles. As an adult, Kevin feels responsible for the emotional well-being of his partners and friends, often neglecting his own needs.

5. Inconsistent or Unpredictable Parenting

PARENTS WHO ARE INCONSISTENT or unpredictable in their behavior can create an environment of uncertainty and anxiety. Children in such environments may develop hyper-vigilance and a need to control their surroundings to feel safe, leading to codependent behaviors.

Example: Rachel's father was loving and attentive at times but could also be harsh and unpredictable. Rachel never knew what to expect from him and learned to be constantly on guard. As an adult, Rachel tries to control her relationships and surroundings to avoid the anxiety of unpredictability.

Role of Trauma and Past Relationships

TRAUMA AND PAST RELATIONSHIPS play a significant role in the development and reinforcement of codependent behaviors. Understanding these influences is crucial for addressing the roots of codependency.

1. Childhood Trauma

CHILDHOOD TRAUMA, SUCH as abuse, neglect, or witnessing domestic violence, can profoundly impact an individual's development and contribute to codependent behaviors. Trauma survivors often struggle with feelings of powerlessness and a need to regain control, leading them to take on caretaking roles in their relationships.

Example: Lisa experienced physical abuse from her father during her childhood. To cope with the trauma, she learned to anticipate his needs and avoid triggering his anger. In her adult relationships, Lisa continues to prioritize others' needs to maintain a sense of control and avoid conflict.

2. Dysfunctional Romantic Relationships

PAST ROMANTIC RELATIONSHIPS can also reinforce codependent patterns. Being involved with partners who are abusive, addicted, or emotionally unavailable can perpetuate feelings of unworthiness and a compulsion to fix or save the other person.

Example: Mark's first serious relationship was with a woman who struggled with addiction. Mark believed he could help her overcome her addiction if he loved her enough. The relationship ended in heartbreak, but Mark continued to seek out partners who needed saving, reinforcing his codependent patterns.

3. Betrayal and Abandonment

EXPERIENCES OF BETRAYAL or abandonment can lead to deep-seated fears of rejection and a heightened need for approval and validation. These experiences can drive codependent behaviors as individuals seek to avoid future pain by maintaining control over their relationships.

Example: Emma's fiancé left her for someone else shortly before their wedding. This betrayal left Emma feeling unworthy and fearful of future abandonment. In subsequent relationships, she became overly accommodating and avoided conflict at all costs to prevent being abandoned again.

4. Repetition Compulsion

REPETITION COMPULSION is a psychological phenomenon where individuals unconsciously recreate past traumatic experiences in an attempt to gain mastery over them. This can lead to repeated patterns of codependency in relationships.

Example: David grew up with a mother who was emotionally manipulative and controlling. As an adult, he found himself in relationships with similar dynamics, unconsciously seeking to resolve the unresolved issues from his childhood by trying to fix or change his partners.

Influence of Societal and Cultural Factors

SOCIETAL AND CULTURAL factors also play a significant role in shaping codependent behaviors. Cultural norms, gender roles, and societal expectations can reinforce and perpetuate codependent patterns.

1. Cultural Norms and Expectations

DIFFERENT CULTURES have varying expectations regarding family roles, caregiving, and individual autonomy. In some cultures, collectivism and family loyalty are highly valued, which can lead to codependent behaviors being normalized and even encouraged.

Example: In many Asian cultures, there is a strong emphasis on filial piety and loyalty to family. While these values are important, they can also lead to codependent behaviors where individuals prioritize family needs over their own well-being.

2. Gender Roles and Stereotypes

TRADITIONAL GENDER roles and stereotypes can contribute to the development of codependent behaviors. Women, in particular, are often socialized to be nurturing, self-sacrificing, and responsible for the emotional well-being of others.

Example: Sarah grew up with the belief that a good wife and mother should always put her family's needs first. As a result, she neglected her own career and personal interests to care for her husband and children, leading to feelings of resentment and loss of self-identity.

3. Media and Pop Culture

MEDIA AND POP CULTURE often portray idealized versions of relationships, emphasizing self-sacrifice and martyrdom as expressions of true love. These portrayals can reinforce codependent behaviors and create unrealistic expectations about relationships.

Example: Romantic movies and TV shows frequently depict characters who go to great lengths to save or change their partners. These narratives can lead individuals to believe that their worth is tied to their ability to fix or save others, perpetuating codependent behaviors.

4. Societal Pressure and Success

SOCIETAL PRESSURE TO succeed and be perfect can also contribute to codependent behaviors. Individuals may feel compelled to maintain a façade of having it all together, leading to a neglect of their own needs and an overemphasis on controlling their environment and relationships.

Example: John felt immense pressure to succeed in his career and maintain a perfect family image. He took on excessive responsibilities at work and home, neglecting his own health and well-being. His need to control everything led to strained relationships and burnout.

Integrating Insights and Moving Forward

RECOGNIZING THE ROOTS of codependency is the first step towards healing and recovery. By understanding the impact of family dynamics, childhood experiences, trauma, past relationships, and societal and cultural factors, individuals can gain insight into their codependent behaviors and begin to address them.

Practical Steps for Healing

1. Therapy and Counseling

SEEKING THERAPY OR counseling can provide a safe space to explore the roots of codependency and develop healthier relationship patterns. Therapists can help individuals understand their past experiences, address unresolved trauma, and learn new coping strategies.

Example: Rachel started seeing a therapist to work through her issues with control and anxiety. Through therapy, she gained insight into how her childhood experiences with her unpredictable father influenced her codependent behaviors. She learned to set boundaries and prioritize her own needs.

2. Support Groups

JOINING SUPPORT GROUPS, such as Codependents Anonymous (CoDA), can provide a sense of community and support from others who are experiencing similar challenges. Sharing experiences and learning from others can be empowering and validating.

Example: Mark joined a Codependents Anonymous group and found it helpful to connect with others who understood his struggles. The support and encouragement from the group helped him feel less alone and more motivated to make positive changes.

3. Self-Reflection and Journaling

ENGAGING IN SELF-REFLECTION and journaling can help individuals gain insight into their thoughts, feelings, and behaviors. Writing about past experiences, current challenges, and future goals can be a powerful tool for personal growth.

Example: Emma started journaling about her experiences of betrayal and abandonment. Through writing, she was able to process her emotions and gain a deeper understanding of how these experiences influenced her codependent behaviors. Journaling helped her develop healthier ways of coping with her fears.

4. Education and Awareness

EDUCATING ONESELF ABOUT codependency and its roots can be empowering. Reading books, attending workshops, and seeking information from reputable sources can provide valuable insights and tools for recovery.

Example: Jane read several books about codependency and attended workshops on healthy relationships. The knowledge she gained helped her recognize her codependent patterns and develop strategies for change. She began to prioritize her own needs and set boundaries with her husband.

5. Mindfulness and Self-Care

PRACTICING MINDFULNESS and self-care is essential for breaking free from codependent patterns. Mindfulness techniques, such as meditation and deep breathing, can help individuals stay present and manage anxiety. Self-care activities, such as exercise, hobbies, and relaxation, can promote well-being and self-worth.

Example: Kevin started practicing mindfulness meditation to manage his anxiety and stay present. He also made a commitment to prioritize self-care by engaging in activities he enjoyed, such as hiking and painting. These practices helped him feel more grounded and less dependent on others for validation.

Conclusion

Understanding the roots of codependency is a crucial step in the journey towards healing and recovery. By exploring the impact of family dynamics, childhood experiences, trauma, past relationships, and societal and cultural factors, individuals can gain insight into their behaviors and begin to address them. Healing from codependency involves therapy, support groups, self-reflection, education, mindfulness, and self-care. With dedication and effort, it is possible to break free from codependent patterns and build healthier, more fulfilling relationships.

Chapter 4: The Impact of Codependency

Codependency can have profound effects on various aspects of a person's life. The impact extends beyond emotional and psychological realms, affecting mental and physical health, relationships, social interactions, and overall life satisfaction. This chapter explores the comprehensive effects of codependency, illustrating the urgency of addressing these patterns and offering insights into the long-term consequences if left unaddressed.

Effects on Mental and Physical Health

CODEPENDENCY OFTEN begins as an emotional and psychological issue, but its effects can quickly ripple out to impact mental and physical health. The stress and strain of codependent behaviors take a toll on both the mind and body.

Mental Health Effects

1. Anxiety and Depression

INDIVIDUALS STRUGGLING with codependency frequently experience high levels of anxiety and depression. The constant worry about others' well-being and the fear of rejection or abandonment can lead to chronic anxiety. Similarly, the feelings of inadequacy, low self-esteem, and unfulfilled needs often result in depression.

Example: Emma feels constant anxiety over her partner's moods and actions, fearing that any conflict might lead to abandonment. Her unrelenting need to please and the pressure to maintain harmony take a toll on her mental health, leading to panic attacks and bouts of depression.

2. Chronic Stress

THE PERPETUAL STATE of vigilance and the burden of responsibility for others' happiness can lead to chronic stress. This stress can manifest in various ways, including insomnia, irritability, and difficulty concentrating.

Example: Mark is always on edge, trying to anticipate and meet his partner's needs. This constant state of alertness leads to chronic stress, making it hard for him to relax or enjoy life.

3. Emotional Exhaustion

CODEPENDENT INDIVIDUALS often experience emotional exhaustion from constantly prioritizing others' needs over their own. This exhaustion can lead to burnout, characterized by feelings of helplessness, hopelessness, and a lack of motivation.

Example: Sarah spends so much time and energy taking care of her alcoholic husband that she feels emotionally drained. She finds it hard to engage in activities she once enjoyed and feels a pervasive sense of fatigue.

4. Loss of Identity

OVER TIME, CODEPENDENT individuals may lose their sense of identity, as they become so enmeshed in others' lives that they neglect their own desires, interests, and goals. This loss of identity can lead to a profound sense of emptiness and confusion about one's purpose.

Example: Kevin has spent years catering to his mother's needs, neglecting his own aspirations. Now, he struggles to identify his own goals and interests, feeling lost and purposeless.

Physical Health Effects

1. Somatic Symptoms

CHRONIC STRESS AND emotional turmoil can manifest as physical symptoms, such as headaches, gastrointestinal issues, and muscle tension. These somatic symptoms are the body's response to prolonged stress and emotional strain.

Example: Maria frequently experiences tension headaches and stomachaches, which doctors have linked to the chronic stress of her codependent behaviors.

2. Weakened Immune System

CHRONIC STRESS CAN weaken the immune system, making codependent individuals more susceptible to illnesses and infections. The body's constant fight-or-flight response drains its resources, leaving it less capable of fighting off disease.

Example: John, who is constantly stressed about managing his family's needs, finds that he falls ill frequently, catching colds and infections more easily than before.

3. High Blood Pressure and Heart Disease

THE ONGOING STRESS and anxiety associated with codependency can lead to high blood pressure and increase the risk of heart disease. The body's stress response involves the release of hormones like adrenaline and cortisol, which, over time, can damage cardiovascular health.

Example: Lisa, who has spent years in a high-stress codependent relationship, was recently diagnosed with high blood pressure, a condition her doctor attributes to chronic stress.

4. Poor Self-Care

CODEPENDENT INDIVIDUALS often neglect their own health and well-being. They may skip regular exercise, eat poorly, and avoid medical checkups because they are too focused on others. This neglect can lead to a range of health issues, from weight gain to more serious conditions like diabetes or heart disease.

Example: Tom rarely takes time for himself, skipping workouts and eating convenience foods while caring for his dependent partner. As a result, he has gained weight and developed pre-diabetic symptoms.

Impact on Relationships and Social Interactions

CODEPENDENCY SIGNIFICANTLY affects relationships and social interactions, often creating imbalanced dynamics that are difficult to sustain healthily. The impact can be seen in various types of relationships, including romantic partnerships, friendships, and family dynamics.

Impact on Romantic Relationships

1. Unbalanced Relationships

IN CODEPENDENT ROMANTIC relationships, one partner often takes on the role of caretaker while the other becomes dependent. This imbalance can lead to resentment and frustration on both sides. The caretaker feels overwhelmed and unappreciated, while the dependent partner may feel smothered and infantilized.

Example: Rachel constantly sacrifices her needs to take care of her boyfriend, who struggles with depression. Over time, she becomes resentful of his lack of effort to improve, while he feels increasingly dependent and incapable.

2. Lack of Boundaries

CODEPENDENT RELATIONSHIPS often lack healthy boundaries, with partners enmeshed in each other's lives. This enmeshment can stifle individuality and personal growth, leading to a sense of suffocation and loss of self.

Example: Emily and her husband share every aspect of their lives, including personal finances and friendships. This lack of boundaries leaves Emily feeling like she has no space for herself and her own needs.

3. Emotional Manipulation

IN SOME CODEPENDENT relationships, manipulation can become a tool for maintaining control. The caretaker may use guilt, fear, or obligation to keep the dependent partner close, while the dependent partner may manipulate through helplessness or neediness.

Example: Sarah uses guilt to keep her husband from leaving the house, reminding him of everything she has done for him. Meanwhile, he manipulates her by acting more helpless than he is, ensuring she continues to take care of him.

Impact on Friendships

1. Over-Involvement

CODEPENDENT INDIVIDUALS may become overly involved in their friends' lives, feeling responsible for their happiness and well-being. This over-involvement can lead to a loss of balance in the friendship, with one person giving significantly more than they receive.

Example: Kevin frequently cancels his own plans to help his friend Laura, who constantly has crises. His over-involvement strains their friendship, as Laura becomes increasingly dependent on Kevin's support.

2. Difficulty Maintaining Friendships

THE INTENSE FOCUS ON one or a few relationships can lead to neglect of other friendships. Codependent individuals may struggle to maintain a broader social network, leading to isolation and a lack of support.

Example: Mark's codependency with his partner leaves him little time or energy to invest in other friendships. Over time, his social circle shrinks, leaving him isolated and without a diverse support network.

3. Resentment and Burnout

THE CARETAKER ROLE can lead to feelings of resentment and burnout. Friends who feel overwhelmed by their responsibilities may withdraw or become resentful of the friend they are caring for, straining or ending the friendship.

Example: Maria feels increasingly resentful of her friend Anna, who relies on her for emotional support. Maria's constant caregiving leads to burnout, and she eventually distances herself from the friendship.

Impact on Family Dynamics

1. Role Rigidity

IN FAMILIES WITH CODEPENDENT dynamics, roles can become rigid and unchanging. One family member may always be the caretaker, while another remains dependent. This rigidity can stifle individual growth and prevent family members from developing healthier dynamics.

Example: John's role as the family caretaker has remained unchanged since his childhood. As an adult, he still feels responsible for his parents' and siblings' well-being, preventing him from pursuing his own life fully.

2. Generational Patterns

CODEPENDENT BEHAVIORS can be passed down through generations, with children learning these patterns from their parents. This transmission can perpetuate dysfunctional dynamics and make it harder for family members to break free from codependency.

Example: Lisa learned codependent behaviors from her mother, who was also the caretaker in her family. Now, Lisa finds herself repeating the same patterns with her own children, struggling to break the cycle.

3. Family Conflict

THE IMBALANCE CREATED by codependent dynamics can lead to conflict within the family. Siblings may resent the caretaker for their perceived favoritism towards the dependent family member, leading to tension and discord.

Example: Tom's siblings resent him for always taking care of their mother, believing he receives more appreciation and attention. This resentment leads to frequent conflicts and strained relationships among the siblings.

Long-Term Consequences if Left Unaddressed

THE LONG-TERM CONSEQUENCES of codependency can be severe, affecting various aspects of an individual's life and well-being. If left unaddressed, codependency can lead to lasting emotional, psychological, and physical issues.

1. Chronic Mental Health Issues

UNADDRESSED CODEPENDENCY can lead to chronic mental health issues such as depression, anxiety disorders, and chronic stress. The ongoing emotional turmoil and strain of maintaining codependent behaviors can exacerbate these conditions, making them harder to treat.

Example: Sarah's ongoing anxiety and depression have worsened over the years due to her unresolved codependency. Her mental health issues have become chronic, requiring long-term therapy and medication.

2. Physical Health Decline

THE PHYSICAL EFFECTS of chronic stress and poor self-care can accumulate over time, leading to serious health problems. Conditions such as hypertension, heart disease, gastrointestinal issues, and weakened immune function can become more severe and harder to manage.

Example: John's neglect of his own health has led to significant weight gain, hypertension, and frequent illnesses. His long-term stress and poor self-care have taken a serious toll on his physical health.

3. Relationship Breakdown

CODEPENDENT RELATIONSHIPS are often unsustainable in the long term. The imbalance, lack of boundaries, and emotional strain can lead to relationship breakdowns, whether in romantic partnerships, friendships, or family dynamics.

Example: Mark's codependent relationship with his partner eventually led to a breakup. The strain of constantly trying to fix his partner's issues and neglecting his own needs became too much to bear.

4. Loss of Personal Fulfillment

UNADDRESSED CODEPENDENCY can prevent individuals from pursuing their own goals and aspirations. The constant focus on others' needs can lead to a loss of personal fulfillment and a sense of wasted potential.

Example: Kevin's long-term codependency with his mother prevented him from pursuing a career he was passionate about. Looking back, he feels a deep sense of regret and unfulfillment for not following his dreams.

5. Perpetuation of Dysfunctional Patterns

WITHOUT INTERVENTION, codependent behaviors can continue to perpetuate dysfunctional patterns in relationships and within families. These patterns can be passed down to future generations, making it harder for family members to develop healthy dynamics.

Example: Lisa's unresolved codependency has led her to raise her children with similar behaviors, continuing the cycle of dysfunction. Her children are beginning to exhibit signs of codependency in their own relationships.

6. Isolation and Loneliness

THE INTENSE FOCUS ON a few relationships and the neglect of a broader social network can lead to isolation and loneliness. Codependent individuals may find themselves without a diverse support system, making it harder to cope with life's challenges.

Example: Emma's codependent behaviors led to the loss of several friendships, leaving her isolated and lonely. She struggles to find support outside her codependent relationship, exacerbating her feelings of loneliness.

Steps Towards Recovery and Healing

ADDRESSING CODEPENDENCY requires a multifaceted approach that includes self-awareness, professional help, and the development of healthier behaviors and relationships. The following steps can help individuals begin their journey towards recovery and healing.

1. Acknowledge the Problem

THE FIRST STEP IN ADDRESSING codependency is acknowledging its presence and impact on one's life. This self-awareness is crucial for initiating change and seeking help.

Example: Sarah finally acknowledged that her anxiety and depression were linked to her codependent behaviors. This realization motivated her to seek therapy and support.

2. Seek Professional Help

THERAPY OR COUNSELING can provide valuable support and guidance in addressing codependency. Therapists can help individuals explore the roots of their behaviors, develop healthier coping strategies, and work through unresolved trauma.

Example: Mark began seeing a therapist who specialized in codependency. Through therapy, he gained insight into his behaviors and learned new ways to manage his anxiety and stress.

3. Build a Support System

Creating a diverse support system is essential for recovery. This can include friends, family members, support groups, and online communities. A strong support system provides encouragement, validation, and accountability.

Example: John joined a Codependents Anonymous group and reconnected with old friends. The support and understanding he received from the group and his friends helped him feel less isolated.

4. Practice Self-Care

PRIORITIZING SELF-CARE is crucial for breaking free from codependent patterns. This includes physical self-care, such as exercise and healthy eating, as well as emotional self-care, such as relaxation and hobbies.

Example: Maria made a commitment to prioritize her own health and well-being. She started exercising regularly, eating healthier, and setting aside time for hobbies she enjoyed.

5. Set Boundaries

LEARNING TO SET AND maintain healthy boundaries is a key aspect of overcoming codependency. Boundaries help protect one's well-being and ensure that relationships are balanced and respectful.

Example: Emily learned to set boundaries with her husband, ensuring that she had time and space for herself. She communicated her needs clearly and assertively, helping to create a more balanced relationship.

6. Focus on Personal Growth

PURSUING PERSONAL GOALS and interests can help individuals build a sense of identity and fulfillment outside of their codependent relationships. This can include career aspirations, educational pursuits, and personal hobbies.

Example: Kevin decided to pursue his passion for writing, enrolling in a creative writing course. This focus on personal growth helped him rediscover his sense of identity and purpose.

7. Develop Healthy Relationship Skills

BUILDING HEALTHY RELATIONSHIPS requires communication, empathy, and mutual respect. Learning and practicing these skills can help individuals create more fulfilling and balanced connections with others.

Example: Lisa attended workshops on healthy relationship skills, learning how to communicate effectively and set boundaries. These skills helped her develop healthier dynamics in her relationships.

Conclusion

The impact of codependency is far-reaching, affecting mental and physical health, relationships, and overall life satisfaction. Understanding these effects underscores the importance of addressing codependent behaviors and seeking recovery. By acknowledging the problem, seeking professional help, building a support system, practicing self-care, setting boundaries, focusing on personal growth, and developing healthy relationship skills, individuals can begin to break free from codependency and build a more fulfilling, balanced life. The journey towards healing may be challenging, but it is achievable and essential for long-term well-being and happiness.

Chapter 5: Breaking the Cycle

Breaking the cycle of codependency is a journey that requires courage, self-awareness, and dedication. It involves acknowledging and accepting the problem, cultivating self-awareness and mindfulness, and implementing practical strategies to develop healthier relationship patterns. This chapter explores each of these steps in depth, providing a comprehensive guide to overcoming codependency.

Acknowledging and Accepting the Problem

THE FIRST STEP IN BREAKING the cycle of codependency is acknowledging and accepting that there is a problem. This step is often the most challenging, as it requires confronting uncomfortable truths about oneself and one's relationships. However, without this crucial first step, meaningful change cannot occur.

1. Recognizing Codependent Behaviors

To acknowledge codependency, it is essential to recognize the behaviors and patterns that characterize it. This includes understanding the emotional, behavioral, and psychological symptoms discussed in previous chapters. Common signs of codependency include excessive caretaking, people-pleasing, difficulty setting boundaries, low self-esteem, and an overreliance on others for validation.

Example: Jane began to notice that she was constantly putting her partner's needs above her own, to the point of neglecting her health and well-being. She realized that her desire to please and avoid conflict was a significant factor in her unhappiness.

2. Reflecting on Personal History

REFLECTING ON ONE'S personal history can provide valuable insights into the roots of codependency. This includes examining family dynamics, childhood experiences, past relationships, and any trauma that may have contributed to the development of codependent behaviors.

Example: Mark spent time reflecting on his childhood, where he often felt responsible for his mother's happiness due to her emotional volatility. He recognized that this early experience influenced his tendency to prioritize others' needs over his own.

3. Accepting Responsibility

ACCEPTING RESPONSIBILITY for one's role in maintaining codependent patterns is crucial for change. This does not mean blaming oneself but rather recognizing that change is possible and that one has the power to make different choices.

Example: Maria acknowledged that while her partner's behavior was problematic, she also played a role by enabling it and neglecting her needs. She accepted that she had the power to change her own behavior and set healthier boundaries.

4. Seeking Support

ACKNOWLEDGING AND ACCEPTING codependency can be an emotionally challenging process. Seeking support from trusted friends, family members, or mental health professionals can provide the encouragement and guidance needed to navigate this journey.

Example: Kevin confided in a close friend about his struggles with codependency. His friend's understanding and support gave him the strength to seek therapy and begin working on his issues.

The Importance of Self-Awareness and Mindfulness

SELF-AWARENESS AND mindfulness are critical tools in breaking the cycle of codependency. They help individuals understand their thoughts, feelings, and behaviors and create a foundation for intentional change.

1. Cultivating Self-Awareness

SELF-AWARENESS INVOLVES a deep understanding of oneself, including one's motivations, triggers, and patterns of behavior. Developing self-awareness can help individuals recognize codependent tendencies and make more conscious choices.

Example: Rachel started journaling regularly to explore her thoughts and emotions. Through this practice, she became more aware of her tendency to seek validation from others and the underlying fears driving this behavior.

2. Practicing Mindfulness

MINDFULNESS IS THE practice of being present and fully engaged in the current moment. It involves observing one's thoughts and feelings without judgment. Mindfulness can help individuals break automatic, codependent reactions and respond to situations more thoughtfully.

Example: John began practicing mindfulness meditation, focusing on his breath and observing his thoughts. This practice helped him become more aware of his anxious thoughts and allowed him to respond to situations with greater calm and clarity.

3. Identifying Triggers

IDENTIFYING TRIGGERS is an essential aspect of self-awareness. Triggers are situations, people, or emotions that provoke codependent behaviors. Recognizing these triggers can help individuals develop strategies to manage them effectively.

Example: Lisa identified that she felt particularly anxious and codependent when dealing with her sister's crises. Recognizing this trigger allowed her to prepare herself mentally and emotionally for these interactions and set clearer boundaries.

4. Developing Emotional Regulation Skills

EMOTIONAL REGULATION involves managing and responding to intense emotions in a healthy way. This includes techniques such as deep breathing, progressive muscle relaxation, and cognitive reframing. These skills can help individuals navigate the emotional challenges of breaking codependent patterns.

Example: Tom learned deep breathing techniques to manage his anxiety when he felt the urge to overextend himself for others. This practice helped him stay calm and make more balanced decisions.

Strategies for Breaking Codependent Patterns

BREAKING CODEPENDENT patterns requires a combination of self-awareness, practical strategies, and ongoing effort. The following strategies can help individuals develop healthier relationship dynamics and build a stronger sense of self.

1. Setting Boundaries

SETTING AND MAINTAINING healthy boundaries is a cornerstone of breaking codependent patterns. Boundaries protect one's well-being and ensure that relationships are balanced and respectful.

Example: Emily learned to set boundaries with her husband by clearly communicating her needs and limits. She started saying no to unreasonable requests and ensuring she had time for her interests and self-care.

Steps to Set Healthy Boundaries:

- IDENTIFY NEEDS AND Limits: Reflect on what you need to feel safe, respected, and valued in your relationships.

- Communicate Clearly: Use assertive communication to express your boundaries to others. Use "I" statements to convey your needs without blaming or accusing.

- Be Consistent: Consistency is key to maintaining boundaries. Follow through with your stated limits and enforce consequences if boundaries are violated.

- Practice Self-Compassion: Setting boundaries can be challenging and may evoke feelings of guilt or anxiety. Practice self-compassion and remind yourself that boundaries are essential for healthy relationships.

2. Building Self-Esteem

BUILDING SELF-ESTEEM is crucial for overcoming codependency. A strong sense of self-worth can help individuals rely less on external validation and make choices that align with their values and needs.

Example: Mark worked on building his self-esteem by acknowledging his accomplishments and strengths. He also challenged negative self-talk and replaced it with positive affirmations.

Strategies for Building Self-Esteem:

- PRACTICE SELF-COMPASSION: Treat yourself with kindness and understanding, especially when you make mistakes or face challenges.

- Celebrate Achievements: Acknowledge and celebrate your accomplishments, no matter how small.

- Challenge Negative Self-Talk: Identify and challenge negative thoughts about yourself. Replace them with positive and realistic affirmations.

- Surround Yourself with Positive Influences: Spend time with people who support and uplift you. Avoid relationships that undermine your self-worth.

3. Prioritizing Self-Care

PRIORITIZING SELF-CARE is essential for breaking codependent patterns. Self-care involves taking deliberate actions to nurture your physical, emotional, and mental well-being.

Example: Maria made self-care a priority by scheduling regular exercise, healthy meals, and relaxation activities. She also set aside time for hobbies and socializing with friends.

Self-Care Strategies:

- PHYSICAL SELF-CARE: Engage in regular exercise, eat a balanced diet, get enough sleep, and attend regular medical checkups.

- Emotional Self-Care: Practice mindfulness, journaling, and activities that bring joy and relaxation.

- Mental Self-Care: Challenge yourself intellectually through reading, learning new skills, or engaging in creative activities.

- Social Self-Care: Spend time with supportive friends and family, and seek out social activities that you enjoy.

4. Developing Healthy Relationship Skills

DEVELOPING HEALTHY relationship skills can help individuals create more balanced and fulfilling connections. This includes communication, empathy, conflict resolution, and mutual respect.

Example: Kevin attended a workshop on healthy relationship skills, where he learned effective communication techniques and strategies for managing conflict. He practiced these skills in his relationships, leading to more positive interactions.

Key Relationship Skills:

- EFFECTIVE COMMUNICATION: Use assertive communication to express your needs and listen actively to others.

- Empathy: Practice empathy by trying to understand and validate others' feelings and perspectives.

- Conflict Resolution: Learn to navigate conflicts constructively by staying calm, addressing issues directly, and seeking win-win solutions.

- Mutual Respect: Foster relationships based on mutual respect, where both parties' needs and boundaries are valued.

5. Rebuilding Personal Identity

REBUILDING PERSONAL identity involves reconnecting with your interests, values, and goals. This process helps individuals develop a sense of self that is independent of their relationships.

Example: Rachel started exploring her interests and passions, such as painting and hiking. She set personal goals and pursued activities that brought her joy and fulfillment.

Steps to Rebuild Personal Identity:

- EXPLORE INTERESTS and Hobbies: Reconnect with activities that you enjoy and explore new interests.

- Set Personal Goals: Identify and pursue goals that align with your values and aspirations.

- Reflect on Values: Consider what values are important to you and how you can live in alignment with them.

- Cultivate Independence: Practice making decisions and taking actions that are based on your needs and desires, rather than others' expectations.

6. Seeking Professional Help

THERAPY OR COUNSELING can provide valuable support and guidance in breaking codependent patterns. Therapists can help individuals explore the roots of their behaviors, develop healthier coping strategies, and work through unresolved trauma.

Example: John sought therapy to address his codependent behaviors. His therapist helped him understand the underlying issues and develop practical strategies for change.

Types of Therapy for Codependency:

- COGNITIVE-BEHAVIORAL Therapy (CBT): CBT focuses on identifying and changing negative thought patterns and behaviors.

- Dialectical Behavior Therapy (DBT): DBT combines cognitive-behavioral techniques with mindfulness practices to help individuals manage emotions and improve relationships.

- Family Therapy: Family therapy can address dysfunctional family dynamics and help family members develop healthier relationships.

- TRAUMA-INFORMED THERAPY: Trauma-informed therapy focuses on understanding and healing the impact of past trauma on current behaviors.

7. Engaging in Support Groups

JOINING SUPPORT GROUPS, such as Codependents Anonymous (CoDA), can provide a sense of community and support from others who are experiencing similar challenges. Sharing experiences and learning from others can be empowering and validating.

Example: Lisa joined a Codependents Anonymous group and found it helpful to connect with others who understood her struggles. The support and encouragement from the group helped her feel less alone and more motivated to make positive changes.

Benefits of Support Groups:

- SHARED EXPERIENCES: Connecting with others who have similar experiences can provide validation and understanding.

- Peer Support: Support groups offer a sense of community and encouragement from others on a similar journey.

- Accountability: Being part of a group can provide accountability and motivation to continue working on personal growth.

- Learning from Others: Support groups provide opportunities to learn from others' experiences and strategies for overcoming codependency.

8. Practicing Gratitude

PRACTICING GRATITUDE can help individuals shift their focus from what is lacking to what is positive in their lives. This practice can improve overall well-being and foster a more positive outlook.

Example: Tom started keeping a gratitude journal, where he wrote down three things he was grateful for each day. This practice helped him appreciate the positive aspects of his life and reduce his focus on negative thoughts.

Gratitude Practices:

- GRATITUDE JOURNAL: Write down things you are grateful for each day, focusing on both big and small positives.

- Expressing Gratitude: Take time to express gratitude to others, whether through verbal acknowledgment, thank-you notes, or acts of kindness.

- Mindfulness Meditation: Incorporate gratitude into mindfulness meditation by focusing on things you are thankful for during your practice.

9. Embracing Self-Compassion

SELF-COMPASSION INVOLVES treating oneself with kindness and understanding, especially in times of difficulty. It helps individuals recognize their inherent worth and reduces the tendency to engage in self-criticism.

Example: Emily practiced self-compassion by acknowledging her efforts and progress, even when things didn't go perfectly. She reminded herself that she deserved kindness and understanding, just like anyone else.

Self-Compassion Practices:

- SELF-KINDNESS: TREAT yourself with the same kindness and care that you would offer to a friend.

- Common Humanity: Recognize that everyone makes mistakes and faces challenges; you are not alone in your struggles.

- Mindful Awareness: Observe your thoughts and feelings without judgment, allowing yourself to experience them without being overwhelmed.

10. Celebrating Progress

RECOGNIZING AND CELEBRATING progress is essential for maintaining motivation and reinforcing positive changes. Celebrating small victories can help individuals see the value in their efforts and stay committed to their journey.

Example: Kevin celebrated his progress by acknowledging each step he took towards healthier relationships and self-care. He rewarded himself with small treats and shared his achievements with supportive friends.

Ways to Celebrate Progress:

- ACKNOWLEDGE ACHIEVEMENTS: Take time to recognize and celebrate each step forward, no matter how small.

- Reward Yourself: Treat yourself to something special as a reward for your efforts and progress.

- Share Successes: Share your achievements with supportive friends or family members who can celebrate with you.

- Reflect on Growth: Regularly reflect on how far you've come and the positive changes you've made.

Conclusion

Breaking the cycle of codependency is a challenging but achievable journey that requires self-awareness, mindfulness, and practical strategies. By acknowledging and accepting the problem, cultivating self-awareness, setting boundaries, building self-esteem, prioritizing self-care, developing healthy relationship skills, rebuilding personal identity, seeking professional help, engaging in support groups, practicing gratitude and self-compassion, and celebrating progress, individuals can develop healthier relationship patterns and build a stronger sense of self. The journey towards healing and recovery is ongoing, but with dedication and effort, it is possible to overcome codependency and create a fulfilling, balanced life.

Chapter 6: Establishing Boundaries

———

Boundaries are the invisible lines that define where one person ends and another begins, delineating personal space, responsibilities, and the extent of one's willingness to engage in various aspects of relationships. For individuals struggling with codependency, establishing and maintaining healthy boundaries can be particularly challenging yet crucial for fostering healthy, balanced relationships. This chapter explores the importance of boundaries, provides techniques for setting and maintaining them, and offers strategies to overcome the guilt and fear often associated with boundary-setting.

Understanding the Importance of Boundaries

BOUNDARIES ARE ESSENTIAL for personal well-being and healthy relationships. They help protect one's physical, emotional, and mental health, enabling individuals to maintain a sense of self while interacting with others. Without clear boundaries, individuals may experience burnout, resentment, and a loss of identity.

1. Protection of Well-Being

BOUNDARIES ACT AS A protective barrier, safeguarding individuals from emotional harm and physical exhaustion. They allow people to prioritize their own needs and well-being, ensuring they have the energy and resources to care for themselves and others.

Example: Jane, a nurse, often found herself overwhelmed by her job and her family's demands. By setting clear boundaries around her work hours and personal time, she was able to protect her well-being and avoid burnout.

2. Maintenance of Identity

BOUNDARIES HELP MAINTAIN a clear sense of identity, preventing individuals from becoming enmeshed in others' lives. They enable individuals to pursue their interests, goals, and values, fostering a strong sense of self.

Example: Mark realized he was losing his sense of identity in his relationship, always prioritizing his partner's needs over his own. By setting boundaries, he was able to reclaim his interests and passions, strengthening his sense of self.

3. Promotion of Healthy Relationships

HEALTHY BOUNDARIES promote mutual respect and understanding in relationships. They ensure that interactions are balanced, with each person's needs and limits being acknowledged and respected.

Example: Maria found that her friendships improved when she set boundaries around how much time she spent helping others. This allowed her to enjoy more balanced, reciprocal relationships.

4. Prevention of Resentment and Burnout

WITHOUT BOUNDARIES, individuals may overextend themselves, leading to resentment and burnout. Boundaries help manage expectations and prevent the emotional toll of constantly prioritizing others over oneself.

Example: Kevin often felt resentful because he was always the one making sacrifices for his family. By setting boundaries, he was able to manage his time and energy better, reducing his feelings of resentment.

Techniques for Setting and Maintaining Healthy Boundaries

SETTING AND MAINTAINING healthy boundaries involves clear communication, self-awareness, and consistent enforcement. The following techniques can help individuals establish boundaries that protect their well-being and foster healthy relationships.

1. Identify Personal Needs and Limits

THE FIRST STEP IN SETTING boundaries is understanding one's needs and limits. This involves self-reflection to identify what is necessary for one's physical, emotional, and mental health.

Example: Rachel took time to reflect on what she needed to feel balanced and fulfilled. She realized that she needed time for herself each day, a reasonable workload, and space from her overly demanding friend.

Steps to Identify Needs and Limits:

- REFLECT ON PAST EXPERIENCES where you felt overwhelmed or taken advantage of. What specific actions or situations contributed to these feelings?

- Consider what you need to feel safe, respected, and valued in your relationships.

- Identify your non-negotiables—things you absolutely need to protect your well-being.

2. Communicate Clearly and Assertively

ONCE NEEDS AND LIMITS are identified, it is essential to communicate them clearly and assertively. Assertive communication involves expressing oneself honestly and respectfully, without aggression or passivity.

Example: John used assertive communication to tell his boss that he could no longer work overtime every week. He explained his need for personal time and how it would improve his productivity.

Tips for Clear and Assertive Communication:

- USE "I" STATEMENTS to express your needs and feelings (e.g., "I need some time to myself each evening to recharge.").

- Be specific about what you need and why it is important.

- Maintain a calm and respectful tone, even if others react negatively.

- Practice active listening, ensuring you also understand and acknowledge others' perspectives.

3. Practice Consistency

CONSISTENCY IS CRUCIAL for maintaining boundaries. Once a boundary is set, it is important to enforce it regularly to ensure it is respected.

Example: Lisa consistently reinforced her boundary of not answering work emails after 6 PM. Over time, her colleagues learned to respect her personal time.

Strategies for Consistency:

- CLEARLY DEFINE WHAT your boundaries are and communicate them to others.

- Follow through with consequences if your boundaries are violated.

- Regularly reassess your boundaries to ensure they still meet your needs.

4. Use Positive Reinforcement

POSITIVE REINFORCEMENT can encourage others to respect your boundaries. Acknowledge and appreciate when others honor your limits.

Example: Tom thanked his friend for understanding when he needed to leave a social event early. This positive reinforcement encouraged his friend to respect his boundaries in the future.

Ways to Use Positive Reinforcement:

- EXPRESS GRATITUDE when others respect your boundaries.

- Highlight the benefits of respecting boundaries, such as improved relationships and reduced stress.

- Provide positive feedback to encourage continued respectful behavior.

5. Seek Support

Setting boundaries can be challenging, especially if others resist or react negatively. Seeking support from trusted friends, family members, or professionals can provide encouragement and guidance.

Example: Emily sought support from a therapist to help her navigate the challenges of setting boundaries with her controlling parents. The therapist provided strategies and reassurance, helping her stay committed to her boundaries.

Sources of Support:

- FRIENDS AND FAMILY members who respect and understand your need for boundaries.

- Support groups, such as Codependents Anonymous, where you can share experiences and learn from others.

- Mental health professionals who can provide guidance and coping strategies.

6. Practice Self-Care

PRIORITIZING SELF-CARE reinforces the importance of boundaries. Taking time to care for oneself can strengthen resolve and provide the energy needed to maintain boundaries.

Example: Kevin made self-care a priority by scheduling regular activities that nurtured his well-being, such as yoga and reading. This practice helped him stay committed to his boundaries.

Self-Care Practices:

- PHYSICAL SELF-CARE: Exercise, healthy eating, sufficient sleep, and regular medical checkups.

- Emotional self-care: Mindfulness, journaling, therapy, and engaging in activities that bring joy.

- Mental self-care: Intellectual stimulation through reading, learning new skills, and creative pursuits.

- Social self-care: Spending time with supportive friends and family, and participating in social activities that you enjoy.

7. Reframe Boundaries as Acts of Love

REFRAMING BOUNDARIES as acts of love, both for oneself and others, can help overcome the guilt often associated with setting limits. Boundaries are not about rejecting others but about ensuring that relationships are healthy and balanced.

Example: Maria reframed her boundary-setting as a way to improve her relationships, recognizing that healthy boundaries allowed her to be more present and engaged with her loved ones.

Ways to Reframe Boundaries:

- RECOGNIZE THAT BOUNDARIES protect your well-being and allow you to be your best self.

- Understand that boundaries foster healthier, more respectful relationships.

- Remind yourself that setting boundaries is an act of self-respect and self-care.

Overcoming Guilt and Fear Associated with Boundary-Setting

MANY INDIVIDUALS STRUGGLE with feelings of guilt and fear when setting boundaries, especially if they are not accustomed to prioritizing their own needs. Overcoming these emotions is essential for establishing and maintaining healthy boundaries.

1. Understand the Root of Guilt and Fear

UNDERSTANDING THE ROOT of guilt and fear can help individuals address these emotions. Guilt often arises from a belief that setting boundaries is selfish or will hurt others, while fear may stem from concerns about rejection or conflict.

Example: Rachel realized her guilt about setting boundaries came from her upbringing, where she was taught that good people always put others first. Her fear of conflict was rooted in past experiences where asserting herself led to arguments.

Strategies to Understand the Root:

- REFLECT ON PAST EXPERIENCES and messages that shaped your beliefs about boundaries.

- Consider how these beliefs influence your current feelings of guilt and fear.

- Recognize that these emotions are common and valid but can be managed.

2. Challenge Negative Beliefs

CHALLENGING NEGATIVE beliefs about boundaries can help reduce feelings of guilt and fear. This involves questioning the validity of these beliefs and replacing them with more positive and realistic perspectives.

Example: John challenged his belief that setting boundaries would make him appear selfish. He reminded himself that taking care of his own needs allowed him to be more effective and supportive in his relationships.

Steps to Challenge Negative Beliefs:

- IDENTIFY NEGATIVE beliefs that contribute to guilt and fear (e.g., "Setting boundaries is selfish").

- Question the accuracy of these beliefs by considering evidence to the contrary.

- Replace negative beliefs with positive affirmations (e.g., "Setting boundaries is an act of self-respect and care").

3. Practice Self-Compassion

SELF-COMPASSION INVOLVES treating oneself with kindness and understanding, especially when facing difficulties. Practicing self-compassion can help individuals navigate the guilt and fear associated with boundary-setting.

Example: Lisa practiced self-compassion by acknowledging that setting boundaries was difficult but necessary for her well-being. She reminded herself that she deserved kindness and understanding, just like anyone else.

Self-Compassion Practices:

- SPEAK TO YOURSELF kindly, as you would to a friend facing similar challenges.

- Acknowledge your efforts and progress, even when things are difficult.

- Allow yourself to feel and process your emotions without judgment.

4. Seek Validation and Support

SEEKING VALIDATION and support from trusted friends, family members, or professionals can help alleviate guilt and fear. Knowing that others understand and support your need for boundaries can provide reassurance and confidence.

Example:

Kevin sought validation from a close friend who had successfully set boundaries in her own life. Her encouragement and understanding helped him feel more confident in his decision to set limits.

Sources of Validation and Support:

- FRIENDS AND FAMILY members who respect and understand your need for boundaries.

- Support groups where you can share experiences and learn from others facing similar challenges.

- Mental health professionals who can provide guidance and reassurance.

5. Take Small Steps

STARTING WITH SMALL, manageable boundaries can help build confidence and reduce feelings of guilt and fear. Gradually increasing the scope of your boundaries allows you to develop skills and experience positive outcomes.

Example: Emily started with small boundaries, such as not answering work calls during dinner. As she became more comfortable, she gradually set more significant limits, like reducing her workload and delegating tasks.

Tips for Taking Small Steps:

- IDENTIFY A SMALL BOUNDARY that feels manageable and start there.

- Practice setting and maintaining this boundary consistently.

- Gradually expand your boundaries as you gain confidence and experience positive results.

6. Focus on the Benefits

FOCUSING ON THE BENEFITS of setting boundaries can help overcome feelings of guilt and fear. Recognize how boundaries improve your well-being, relationships, and overall quality of life.

Example: Tom focused on the benefits of setting boundaries, such as increased energy, better mental health, and more fulfilling relationships. This perspective helped him stay motivated and overcome his initial guilt.

Benefits to Focus On:

- IMPROVED PHYSICAL and emotional well-being.

- More balanced and respectful relationships.

- Increased time and energy for personal interests and goals.

- Enhanced sense of identity and self-worth.

7. Learn from Experience

LEARNING FROM EXPERIENCE involves reflecting on your boundary-setting efforts and adjusting as needed. Recognizing what works and what doesn't can help you refine your approach and build confidence.

Example: Maria reflected on her experiences with boundary-setting, noting what strategies were effective and where she struggled. She used this insight to adjust her approach and improve her skills.

Steps to Learn from Experience:

- REFLECT ON YOUR BOUNDARY-setting efforts, noting successes and challenges.

- Identify what strategies were effective and what needs adjustment.

- Use this insight to refine your approach and continue improving your boundary-setting skills.

Conclusion

Establishing and maintaining healthy boundaries is essential for personal well-being and balanced relationships. By understanding the importance of boundaries, using techniques for setting and maintaining them, and overcoming the guilt and fear associated with boundary-setting, individuals can develop healthier relationship dynamics and build a stronger sense of self. The journey to establishing boundaries may be challenging, but with dedication and effort, it is possible to create a fulfilling, balanced life where one's needs and limits are respected and valued.

Chapter 7: Building Self-Esteem

Self-esteem, or the sense of self-worth and value, plays a pivotal role in our mental and emotional well-being. For individuals struggling with codependency, self-esteem is often compromised, leading to a cycle of unhealthy relationships and behaviors. This chapter delves into the relationship between self-esteem and codependency, provides exercises and activities to boost self-esteem, and offers strategies for overcoming negative self-talk and self-doubt.

The Relationship Between Self-Esteem and Codependency

SELF-ESTEEM IS THE foundation of how we perceive ourselves and interact with the world. It influences our thoughts, emotions, and behaviors. For codependent individuals, low self-esteem is both a cause and a consequence of their behavior patterns.

1. Codependency and Low Self-Esteem

LOW SELF-ESTEEM IS a core component of codependency. Individuals with low self-esteem often feel unworthy, inadequate, and dependent on others for validation. This dependency on external validation can drive codependent behaviors, such as excessive caretaking, people-pleasing, and difficulty setting boundaries.

Example: Jane's low self-esteem made her feel unworthy of love unless she constantly took care of others. This belief led her to neglect her own needs and prioritize her partner's well-being to an unhealthy extent.

2. The Cycle of Codependency and Self-Esteem

THE RELATIONSHIP BETWEEN self-esteem and codependency is cyclical. Low self-esteem drives codependent behaviors, which in turn reinforce feelings of inadequacy and worthlessness. For example, constantly sacrificing one's needs for others can lead to burnout, resentment, and further erosion of self-esteem.

Example: Mark's codependent behavior of always putting others first led to exhaustion and resentment. As he became more burned out, his feelings of inadequacy increased, reinforcing his low self-esteem and perpetuating the cycle.

3. Impact on Relationships

LOW SELF-ESTEEM AFFECTS relationships by creating imbalances and unhealthy dynamics. Codependent individuals may become overly reliant on their partners for validation, leading to a loss of identity and an inability to maintain healthy, balanced relationships.

Example: Maria's low self-esteem caused her to seek constant validation from her partner. This dependency created an imbalance in their relationship, with Maria losing her sense of self and becoming increasingly enmeshed in her partner's life.

Exercises and Activities to Boost Self-Esteem

BOOSTING SELF-ESTEEM involves cultivating a positive self-image, developing self-compassion, and engaging in activities that reinforce a sense of worth and value. The following exercises and activities can help individuals build and maintain healthy self-esteem.

1. Self-Compassion Practices

SELF-COMPASSION INVOLVES treating oneself with the same kindness and understanding one would offer a friend. Practicing self-compassion can help individuals develop a more positive and accepting view of themselves.

Example: Lisa practiced self-compassion by acknowledging her efforts and progress, even when things didn't go perfectly. She reminded herself that everyone makes mistakes and deserves kindness.

Self-Compassion Exercises:

- SELF-COMPASSION MEDITATION: Engage in guided meditations that focus on self-compassion and kindness.

- Compassionate Letter: Write a letter to yourself, offering understanding and support as you would to a friend facing similar challenges.

- Affirmations: Create and repeat positive affirmations that emphasize self-acceptance and worth.

2. Gratitude Journaling

GRATITUDE JOURNALING involves writing down things you are grateful for each day. This practice can shift focus from negative thoughts to positive aspects of life, fostering a more positive self-image.

Example: John started a gratitude journal, noting three things he was grateful for each day. This practice helped him appreciate the positive aspects of his life and reduce his focus on negative thoughts.

Gratitude Journal Prompts:

- LIST THREE THINGS you are grateful for today.

- Reflect on a positive experience you had recently and why it was meaningful.

- Write about a personal strength or quality you are proud of and how it has positively impacted your life.

3. Affirmations and Positive Self-Talk

AFFIRMATIONS ARE POSITIVE statements that can help challenge and overcome negative thoughts. Repeating affirmations can reinforce a positive self-image and boost self-esteem.

Example: Maria used affirmations to counteract her negative self-talk. She repeated statements like "I am worthy of love and respect" and "I am capable and strong" to build her self-esteem.

Examples of Affirmations:

- I AM WORTHY OF LOVE and respect.

- I am capable and strong.

- I deserve happiness and fulfillment.

- I trust in my abilities and decisions.

- I am proud of who I am becoming.

4. Setting and Achieving Goals

SETTING AND ACHIEVING personal goals can enhance self-esteem by providing a sense of accomplishment and purpose. Goals should be specific, measurable, achievable, relevant, and time-bound (SMART).

Example: Kevin set a goal to complete a creative writing course. Achieving this goal boosted his confidence and reinforced his sense of capability and worth.

Steps to Set and Achieve Goals:

- IDENTIFY A GOAL THAT is meaningful and achievable.

- Break the goal into smaller, manageable steps.

- Create a timeline for achieving each step.

- Celebrate each milestone and reflect on your progress.

5. Engaging in Hobbies and Interests

ENGAGING IN HOBBIES and interests can provide joy, relaxation, and a sense of accomplishment. Pursuing activities that bring pleasure and fulfillment can reinforce a positive self-image.

Example: Emily rediscovered her love for painting and made time for it each week. This creative outlet brought her joy and a sense of achievement, boosting her self-esteem.

Ideas for Hobbies and Interests:

- CREATIVE ACTIVITIES such as painting, writing, or crafting.

- Physical activities like hiking, dancing, or yoga.

- Intellectual pursuits such as reading, learning a new language, or playing chess.

- Social activities like joining a club, volunteering, or attending events.

6. Practicing Self-Care

PRIORITIZING SELF-CARE reinforces the importance of one's well-being and worth. Regular self-care activities can improve physical, emotional, and mental health, contributing to higher self-esteem.

Example: Tom made self-care a priority by scheduling regular exercise, healthy meals, and relaxation activities. This practice helped him feel more balanced and valued.

Self-Care Activities:

- PHYSICAL SELF-CARE: Exercise, healthy eating, sufficient sleep, and regular medical checkups.

- Emotional self-care: Mindfulness, journaling, therapy, and engaging in activities that bring joy.

- Mental self-care: Intellectual stimulation through reading, learning new skills, and creative pursuits.

- Social self-care: Spending time with supportive friends and family, and participating in social activities that you enjoy.

7. Volunteering and Helping Others

VOLUNTEERING AND HELPING others can boost self-esteem by providing a sense of purpose and fulfillment. Contributing to the well-being of others can reinforce one's value and capabilities.

Example: Lisa volunteered at a local animal shelter, finding joy and fulfillment in helping animals in need. This experience boosted her self-esteem and provided a sense of purpose.

Ways to Volunteer and Help Others:

- VOLUNTEER AT LOCAL charities, shelters, or community organizations.

- Offer your skills and expertise to those in need.

- Participate in community service projects or events.

- Support friends and family through acts of kindness and assistance.

8. Building and Maintaining Supportive Relationships

BUILDING AND MAINTAINING supportive relationships can provide validation, encouragement, and a sense of belonging. Surrounding oneself with positive influences can reinforce self-worth and boost self-esteem.

Example: Kevin built a network of supportive friends who encouraged and uplifted him. Their validation and support helped him feel valued and confident.

Tips for Building Supportive Relationships:

- SEEK OUT INDIVIDUALS who are positive, encouraging, and respectful.

- Nurture existing relationships by spending quality time and expressing appreciation.

- Communicate openly and honestly with friends and family.

- Set boundaries with individuals who undermine your self-esteem.

Overcoming Negative Self-Talk and Self-Doubt

NEGATIVE SELF-TALK and self-doubt are significant barriers to building self-esteem. Overcoming these challenges involves recognizing and challenging negative thoughts, developing healthier thought patterns, and fostering a more positive self-image.

1. Recognizing Negative Self-Talk

THE FIRST STEP IN OVERCOMING negative self-talk is recognizing it. Negative self-talk often involves harsh criticism, self-blame, and catastrophic thinking.

Example: Maria noticed that she frequently engaged in negative self-talk, telling herself that she was not good enough or that she would fail. Recognizing these patterns was the first step towards change.

Common Forms of Negative Self-Talk:

- ALL-OR-NOTHING THINKING: Viewing situations in black-and-white terms, without recognizing any middle ground (e.g., "I always mess up").

- Catastrophizing: Expecting the worst possible outcome (e.g., "If I make a mistake, it will be a disaster").

- Personalization: Blaming oneself for events outside of one's control (e.g., "It's my fault that my friend is upset").

- Should Statements: Placing unrealistic demands on oneself (e.g., "I should always be perfect").

2. Challenging Negative Thoughts

CHALLENGING NEGATIVE thoughts involves questioning their validity and replacing them with more positive and realistic perspectives. This process can help reduce the impact of negative self-talk and build self-esteem.

Example: John challenged his negative thought, "I'm not good enough," by listing his achievements and strengths. This helped him develop a more balanced and positive self-view.

Steps to Challenge Negative Thoughts:

- IDENTIFY THE NEGATIVE thought and its underlying belief.

- Question the accuracy of the thought by considering evidence to the contrary.

- Replace the negative thought with a positive and realistic affirmation.

- Practice this process regularly to reinforce healthier thought patterns.

3. Developing a Growth Mindset

A GROWTH MINDSET INVOLVES viewing challenges and setbacks as opportunities for learning and growth. Developing a growth mindset can reduce self-doubt and foster a more positive self-image.

Example: Kevin adopted a growth mindset by viewing his mistakes as learning opportunities. This perspective helped him approach challenges with confidence and resilience.

Ways to Develop a Growth Mindset:

- EMBRACE CHALLENGES as opportunities to learn and grow.

- View mistakes and setbacks as part of the learning process.

- Focus on effort and progress rather than perfection.

- Celebrate small victories and milestones along the way.

4. Practicing Mindfulness and Meditation

MINDFULNESS AND MEDITATION can help individuals become more aware of their thoughts and reduce the impact of negative self-talk. These practices encourage present-moment awareness and non-judgmental observation of thoughts and feelings.

Example: Lisa practiced mindfulness meditation to become more aware of her negative self-talk. This practice helped her observe her thoughts without judgment and respond more calmly.

Mindfulness and Meditation Practices:

- MINDFULNESS MEDITATION: Focus on your breath and observe your thoughts and feelings without judgment.

- Body Scan Meditation: Pay attention to different parts of your body, noticing any sensations and allowing them to be.

- Loving-Kindness Meditation: Cultivate feelings of compassion and kindness towards yourself and others.

5. Seeking Professional Help

THERAPY OR COUNSELING can provide valuable support and guidance in overcoming negative self-talk and self-doubt. Mental health professionals can help individuals explore the roots of their negative thoughts and develop healthier thought patterns.

Example: Tom sought therapy to address his negative self-talk and self-doubt. His therapist provided strategies and exercises to challenge negative thoughts and build self-esteem.

Types of Therapy for Negative Self-Talk:

- COGNITIVE-BEHAVIORAL Therapy (CBT): CBT focuses on identifying and changing negative thought patterns and behaviors.

- Dialectical Behavior Therapy (DBT): DBT combines cognitive-behavioral techniques with mindfulness practices to help individuals manage emotions and improve relationships.

- Self-Compassion Therapy: This therapy focuses on developing self-compassion and reducing self-criticism.

6. Building a Support Network

BUILDING A SUPPORT network of positive and encouraging individuals can provide validation and reinforcement for positive self-talk. Supportive relationships can help individuals challenge negative thoughts and build self-esteem.

Example: Emily built a network of supportive friends who provided encouragement and validation. Their positive feedback helped her challenge her negative self-talk and build confidence.

Tips for Building a Support Network:

- SEEK OUT INDIVIDUALS who are positive, encouraging, and respectful.

- Nurture existing relationships by spending quality time and expressing appreciation.

- Communicate openly and honestly with friends and family.

- Set boundaries with individuals who undermine your self-esteem.

7. Practicing Self-Acceptance

SELF-ACCEPTANCE INVOLVES embracing oneself fully, including strengths and weaknesses. Practicing self-acceptance can reduce self-doubt and foster a more positive self-image.

Example: John practiced self-acceptance by acknowledging his imperfections and embracing them as part of who he was. This helped him feel more confident and less critical of himself.

Ways to Practice Self-Acceptance:

- ACKNOWLEDGE AND ACCEPT your strengths and weaknesses.

- Practice self-compassion and kindness towards yourself.

- Avoid comparing yourself to others and focus on your unique qualities.

- Celebrate your individuality and embrace your authentic self.

8. Engaging in Positive Activities

ENGAGING IN ACTIVITIES that bring joy and fulfillment can reinforce a positive self-image and reduce the impact of negative self-talk. These activities provide opportunities for positive experiences and self-expression.

Example: Maria engaged in activities she enjoyed, such as hiking and painting. These positive experiences helped her feel more confident and reduce her focus on negative thoughts.

Ideas for Positive Activities:

- CREATIVE ACTIVITIES such as painting, writing, or crafting.

- Physical activities like hiking, dancing, or yoga.

- Intellectual pursuits such as reading, learning a new language, or playing chess.

- Social activities like joining a club, volunteering, or attending events.

Conclusion

Building self-esteem is essential for overcoming codependency and fostering healthier relationships and a stronger sense of self. By understanding the relationship between self-esteem and codependency, engaging in exercises and activities to boost self-esteem, and overcoming negative self-talk and self-doubt, individuals can develop a positive self-image and break the cycle of codependency. The journey to building self-esteem may be challenging, but with dedication and effort, it is possible to create a fulfilling, balanced life where one's worth and value are recognized and celebrated.

Chapter 8: Developing Healthy Relationships

Developing healthy relationships is essential for personal well-being and happiness. For individuals struggling with codependency, shifting from unhealthy, imbalanced relationships to healthy, balanced ones can be transformative. This chapter explores the characteristics of healthy versus codependent relationships, essential communication skills and conflict resolution strategies, and ways to build mutual respect and trust.

Characteristics of Healthy Versus Codependent Relationships

UNDERSTANDING THE DIFFERENCES between healthy and codependent relationships is crucial for recognizing and fostering positive relationship dynamics.

1. Independence and Interdependence

IN HEALTHY RELATIONSHIPS, individuals maintain their independence while also engaging in interdependence. This balance allows partners to support each other without losing their sense of self.

Example: In a healthy relationship, Jane and Mark pursue their interests and goals independently while supporting each other's endeavors. They spend time together and apart, ensuring that both their individual and shared needs are met.

In contrast, codependent relationships often lack this balance. One or both partners may become overly reliant on the other, leading to enmeshment and a loss of individuality.

Example: In a codependent relationship, Maria feels unable to make decisions without her partner's approval. She sacrifices her interests and goals to meet her partner's needs, losing her sense of self in the process.

2. Healthy Boundaries

HEALTHY RELATIONSHIPS are characterized by clear and respectful boundaries. Partners understand and respect each other's limits, ensuring that both individuals feel safe and valued.

Example: Kevin and Lisa set boundaries around their personal time and space. They communicate their needs openly and respect each other's limits, fostering a sense of security and respect.

In codependent relationships, boundaries are often blurred or nonexistent. This lack of boundaries can lead to over-involvement, resentment, and emotional exhaustion.

Example: In a codependent relationship, Tom feels overwhelmed because he is always available to his partner, even when it infringes on his personal time. He struggles to set boundaries, leading to burnout and resentment.

3. Mutual Respect and Trust

MUTUAL RESPECT AND trust are foundational to healthy relationships. Partners value each other's perspectives, feelings, and needs, and trust is built through consistent and honest behavior.

Example: John and Emily trust each other and value each other's opinions. They communicate openly and honestly, building a strong foundation of mutual respect and trust.

In codependent relationships, respect and trust may be compromised. One partner may dominate the relationship, leading to an imbalance of power and trust issues.

Example: In a codependent relationship, Sarah feels she must always agree with her partner to avoid conflict. This dynamic undermines mutual respect and trust, leading to an unhealthy power imbalance.

4. Effective Communication

HEALTHY RELATIONSHIPS are built on effective communication. Partners express their thoughts and feelings openly, listen actively, and resolve conflicts constructively.

Example: Kevin and Lisa practice effective communication by discussing their needs and concerns openly. They listen to each other without interruption and work together to find solutions to conflicts.

In codependent relationships, communication is often poor. Partners may avoid discussing their needs or feelings to prevent conflict, leading to misunderstandings and unresolved issues.

Example: In a codependent relationship, Tom avoids talking about his feelings to keep the peace. This lack of communication leads to unresolved issues and growing resentment.

5. Emotional Support and Empathy

HEALTHY RELATIONSHIPS involve providing and receiving emotional support and practicing empathy. Partners validate each other's feelings and offer comfort during difficult times.

Example: John supports Emily through a challenging work project by listening to her concerns and offering encouragement. Emily feels understood and valued, strengthening their emotional connection.

In codependent relationships, emotional support may be one-sided or conditional. One partner may feel responsible for the other's emotions, leading to an imbalance of support.

Example: In a codependent relationship, Maria feels solely responsible for her partner's happiness. She neglects her own emotional needs, leading to an unhealthy dynamic of one-sided support.

6. Equality and Reciprocity

HEALTHY RELATIONSHIPS are characterized by equality and reciprocity. Partners contribute equally to the relationship and support each other's growth and well-being.

Example: Jane and Mark share responsibilities and decision-making equally. They support each other's personal and professional growth, ensuring that both partners feel valued and fulfilled.

In codependent relationships, equality and reciprocity are often lacking. One partner may take on the majority of responsibilities, leading to an imbalance of effort and support.

Example: In a codependent relationship, Sarah feels burdened by her partner's dependence on her. She takes on most of the responsibilities, leading to an unequal and unsustainable dynamic.

Communication Skills and Conflict Resolution

EFFECTIVE COMMUNICATION and conflict resolution skills are essential for developing and maintaining healthy relationships. These skills enable partners to express their needs, resolve disagreements constructively, and strengthen their connection.

1. Active Listening**

ACTIVE LISTENING INVOLVES fully focusing on the speaker, understanding their message, and responding thoughtfully. This skill fosters empathy and understanding in relationships.

Example: Kevin practices active listening by giving his full attention to Lisa when she speaks. He maintains eye contact, nods in acknowledgment, and asks clarifying questions to ensure he understands her perspective.

Steps for Active Listening:

- GIVE YOUR FULL ATTENTION to the speaker, avoiding distractions.

- Maintain eye contact and use nonverbal cues to show you are listening.

- Reflect back what you have heard to confirm understanding (e.g., "It sounds like you're saying...").

- Avoid interrupting or offering solutions unless asked.

2. Assertive Communication

ASSERTIVE COMMUNICATION involves expressing one's thoughts, feelings, and needs clearly and respectfully. This style of communication promotes honesty and mutual respect.

Example: Lisa uses assertive communication to express her needs to Kevin. She says, "I need some quiet time in the evenings to recharge," clearly stating her need without blaming or criticizing.

Tips for Assertive Communication:

- USE "I" STATEMENTS to express your feelings and needs (e.g., "I feel...when...").

- Be clear and specific about what you need or want.

- Maintain a calm and respectful tone, even if the conversation is difficult.

- Practice active listening to understand the other person's perspective.

3. Nonverbal Communication

NONVERBAL COMMUNICATION, such as body language, facial expressions, and tone of voice, plays a significant role in conveying messages and emotions. Being aware of nonverbal cues can enhance communication.

Example: John is mindful of his nonverbal communication when talking to Emily. He maintains an open posture, uses a warm tone of voice, and smiles to convey his support and understanding.

Nonverbal Communication Tips:

- BE AWARE OF YOUR BODY language and how it may be perceived.

- Use facial expressions and gestures to convey empathy and understanding.

- Pay attention to the other person's nonverbal cues to gain insight into their emotions.

- Ensure that your nonverbal communication aligns with your verbal message.

4. Conflict Resolution

CONFLICT IS A NATURAL part of any relationship, and resolving conflicts constructively is crucial for maintaining a healthy dynamic. Effective conflict resolution involves addressing issues directly and collaboratively.

Example: Jane and Mark use conflict resolution strategies to address disagreements. They discuss their perspectives calmly, seek to understand each other's viewpoints, and work together to find a solution that meets both their needs.

Steps for Effective Conflict Resolution:

- IDENTIFY THE ISSUE clearly and specifically.

- Express your feelings and needs using "I" statements.

- Listen actively to the other person's perspective.

- Brainstorm possible solutions together, focusing on win-win outcomes.

- Agree on a solution and commit to implementing it.

- Follow up to ensure the solution is working and make adjustments if needed.

5. Emotional Regulation

EMOTIONAL REGULATION involves managing and responding to emotions in a healthy way. This skill is essential for handling conflicts and maintaining effective communication.

Example: Kevin practices emotional regulation by taking deep breaths and pausing before responding during heated discussions. This helps him stay calm and respond thoughtfully rather than react impulsively.

Techniques for Emotional Regulation:

- DEEP BREATHING EXERCISES to calm the nervous system.

- Taking a break if emotions become overwhelming, and returning to the conversation when calmer.

- Practicing mindfulness to stay present and aware of your emotions.

- Reflecting on the situation and your feelings before responding.

6. Empathy and Validation

EMPATHY AND VALIDATION involve understanding and acknowledging the other person's feelings and experiences. These skills foster emotional connection and mutual respect.

Example: Lisa practices empathy and validation by acknowledging Kevin's feelings during discussions. She says, "I can see why you're upset, and I understand how that must feel," showing that she values his perspective.

Steps for Practicing Empathy and Validation:

- PUT YOURSELF IN THE other person's shoes and try to understand their perspective.

- Acknowledge their feelings and experiences without judgment.

- Reflect back what you have heard to show understanding (e.g., "It sounds like you're feeling...").

- Offer support and reassurance, even if you don't fully agree with their perspective.

Building Mutual Respect and Trust

MUTUAL RESPECT AND trust are the foundation of healthy relationships. Building and maintaining these qualities involves consistent, honest behavior and a commitment to valuing each other's perspectives and needs.

1. Consistency and Reliability

BEING CONSISTENT AND reliable in your actions and words helps build trust. When partners know they can depend on each other, it fosters a sense of security and mutual respect.

Example: John builds trust with Emily by following through on his commitments. When he promises to help with a project, he ensures he is available and reliable, reinforcing her trust in him.

Tips for Consistency and Reliability:

- FOLLOW THROUGH ON promises and commitments.

- Communicate openly and honestly about your intentions and actions.

- Be dependable and show up for your partner in meaningful ways.

- Acknowledge and address any lapses in consistency to rebuild trust.

2. Honesty and Transparency

HONESTY AND TRANSPARENCY are crucial for building trust and mutual respect. Being open about your thoughts, feelings, and experiences fosters a deeper connection and understanding.

Example: Maria practices honesty and transparency by sharing her feelings and experiences with her partner. She is open about her needs and concerns, building a foundation of trust and respect.

Ways to Practice Honesty and Transparency:

- COMMUNICATE OPENLY about your feelings and experiences.

- Share your thoughts and perspectives honestly, even if they are difficult.

- Be transparent about your intentions and actions.

- Address issues and concerns directly rather than avoiding or hiding them.

3. Respecting Boundaries

RESPECTING EACH OTHER'S boundaries is essential for maintaining mutual respect. This involves understanding and honoring each other's limits and needs.

Example: Kevin respects Lisa's boundaries by giving her space when she needs it. He acknowledges her need for alone time and supports her in taking care of her well-being.

Steps for Respecting Boundaries:

- COMMUNICATE YOUR BOUNDARIES clearly and respectfully.

- Listen to and honor your partner's boundaries.

- Check in regularly to ensure boundaries are being respected.

- Be willing to adjust your behavior to support your partner's needs.

4. Support and Encouragement

PROVIDING SUPPORT AND encouragement helps build mutual respect and trust. Celebrating each other's successes and offering support during challenges fosters a strong and positive connection.

Example: Lisa supports Kevin by celebrating his achievements and offering encouragement during difficult times. Her consistent support strengthens their bond and mutual respect.

Ways to Provide Support and Encouragement:

- CELEBRATE YOUR PARTNER'S successes and achievements.

- Offer encouragement and reassurance during challenges.

- Show empathy and understanding in difficult times.

- Be a source of strength and positivity for each other.

5. Valuing Each Other's Perspectives

VALUING EACH OTHER'S perspectives involves recognizing and appreciating the unique viewpoints and experiences that each partner brings to the relationship. This fosters mutual respect and a deeper understanding.

Example: John values Emily's perspective by actively seeking her input and considering her views in decision-making. He appreciates her unique insights and experiences, strengthening their mutual respect.

Tips for Valuing Each Other's Perspectives:

- ACTIVELY LISTEN TO your partner's viewpoints and experiences.

- Show appreciation for their unique insights and contributions.

- Consider their perspective in decision-making and problem-solving.

- Acknowledge and validate their feelings and experiences.

6. Building Emotional Intimacy

EMOTIONAL INTIMACY involves sharing your innermost thoughts, feelings, and experiences with your partner. This deep level of connection fosters trust, understanding, and mutual respect.

Example: Maria and her partner build emotional intimacy by sharing their fears, dreams, and vulnerabilities with each other. This deep level of sharing strengthens their trust and connection.

Steps to Build Emotional Intimacy:

- SHARE YOUR THOUGHTS, feelings, and experiences openly with your partner.

- Create a safe and supportive environment for sharing.

- Be vulnerable and honest about your fears and insecurities.

- Practice empathy and validation to understand and support each other.

7. Practicing Forgiveness

FORGIVENESS IS AN ESSENTIAL component of building mutual respect and trust. It involves letting go of past hurts and moving forward with a commitment to learning and growth.

Example: Kevin practices forgiveness by letting go of past grievances and focusing on the present. He acknowledges his partner's efforts to change and grow, reinforcing their mutual respect.

Steps for Practicing Forgiveness:

- ACKNOWLEDGE AND ADDRESS the hurt or issue honestly and openly.

- Let go of resentment and focus on healing and moving forward.

- Recognize your partner's efforts to change and grow.

- Commit to learning from past experiences and building a stronger relationship.

Conclusion

Developing healthy relationships involves understanding the characteristics of healthy versus codependent relationships, practicing effective communication and conflict resolution skills, and building mutual respect and trust. By fostering independence, setting healthy boundaries, communicating openly and honestly, and supporting each other's growth and well-being, individuals can create fulfilling and balanced relationships. The journey to developing healthy relationships may be challenging, but with dedication and effort, it is possible to break free from codependent patterns and build a life filled with meaningful, positive connections.

Chapter 9: Embracing Independence

Independence is a cornerstone of personal well-being and healthy relationships. For individuals struggling with codependency, learning to embrace independence can be transformative. This chapter explores the importance of self-reliance and independence, offers guidance on cultivating hobbies and interests outside of relationships, and provides strategies for balancing autonomy and intimacy.

The Importance of Self-Reliance and Independence

SELF-RELIANCE AND INDEPENDENCE are crucial for personal development and the maintenance of healthy relationships. They enable individuals to pursue their goals, build self-esteem, and engage in relationships from a place of strength and self-sufficiency.

1. Building Self-Esteem

INDEPENDENCE FOSTERS self-esteem by allowing individuals to achieve their goals and solve their problems. When people rely on themselves, they develop a sense of competence and confidence.

Example: Jane began setting personal goals and working towards them independently. Achieving these goals, such as learning a new language and completing a marathon, boosted her self-esteem and made her feel more capable.

Benefits of Building Self-Esteem through Independence:

- INCREASED CONFIDENCE in one's abilities.

- A stronger sense of self-worth and value.

- Reduced dependence on others for validation and support.

- Enhanced motivation to pursue personal goals.

2. Enhancing Decision-Making Skills

INDEPENDENCE INVOLVES making decisions based on one's values, needs, and desires. This practice enhances decision-making skills and empowers individuals to take control of their lives.

Example: Mark started making decisions about his career and personal life without seeking approval from others. This practice helped him develop stronger decision-making skills and feel more in control of his future.

Strategies for Enhancing Decision-Making Skills:

- REFLECT ON YOUR VALUES and priorities when making decisions.

- Consider the potential outcomes and consequences of your choices.

- Trust your intuition and judgment.

- Learn from past experiences to improve future decisions.

3. Reducing Emotional Dependence

EMBRACING INDEPENDENCE reduces emotional dependence on others. Individuals learn to manage their emotions and find fulfillment within themselves, rather than relying on external sources for happiness.

Example: Maria practiced emotional self-care by journaling and meditating. These practices helped her manage her emotions independently and reduce her reliance on her partner for emotional support.

Ways to Reduce Emotional Dependence:

- DEVELOP HEALTHY COPING strategies for managing stress and emotions.

- Practice self-care activities that nurture your emotional well-being.

- Build a strong support network of friends and family.

- Seek therapy or counseling to address underlying emotional issues.

4. Promoting Personal Growth

INDEPENDENCE PROMOTES personal growth by encouraging individuals to explore their interests, develop new skills, and pursue their passions. This growth fosters a sense of fulfillment and purpose.

Example: Kevin pursued his passion for photography by taking classes and participating in photography clubs. This pursuit helped him grow personally and professionally, providing a sense of purpose and fulfillment.

Steps to Promote Personal Growth:

- IDENTIFY YOUR INTERESTS and passions.

- Set personal and professional goals that align with your interests.

- Seek opportunities for learning and development.

- Reflect on your progress and celebrate your achievements.

5. Strengthening Relationships

HEALTHY RELATIONSHIPS are built on a foundation of mutual respect and independence. When individuals embrace independence, they bring their strengths and self-sufficiency into their relationships, creating a balanced and supportive dynamic.

Example: Lisa and John maintained their independence by pursuing their interests and goals. This practice strengthened their relationship by allowing them to support each other's growth and maintain a healthy balance.

Benefits of Independence in Relationships:

- REDUCED PRESSURE ON the relationship to fulfill all emotional and practical needs.

- Greater appreciation for each other's individuality and strengths.

- Enhanced ability to support each other's personal growth.

- Increased resilience and stability in the relationship.

Cultivating Hobbies and Interests Outside of Relationships

CULTIVATING HOBBIES and interests outside of relationships is essential for maintaining independence and personal fulfillment. Engaging in activities that bring joy and satisfaction helps individuals build a rich and diverse life.

1. Exploring Interests and Passions

EXPLORING INTERESTS and passions involves identifying activities that bring joy, excitement, and fulfillment. These pursuits provide opportunities for self-expression and personal growth.

Example: Jane explored her interest in gardening by joining a community garden group. This activity brought her joy and satisfaction, allowing her to express her creativity and connect with others who shared her passion.

Steps to Explore Interests and Passions:

- REFLECT ON ACTIVITIES that bring you joy and satisfaction.

- Try new activities and experiences to discover new interests.

- Join clubs, groups, or classes related to your interests.

- Dedicate regular time to pursue your hobbies and passions.

2. Developing Skills and Talents

DEVELOPING SKILLS AND talents involves honing your abilities and pursuing mastery in areas of interest. This practice fosters a sense of accomplishment and boosts self-esteem.

Example: Mark developed his cooking skills by taking culinary classes and experimenting with new recipes. This pursuit not only enhanced his abilities but also provided a sense of accomplishment and pride.

Tips for Developing Skills and Talents:

- SET SPECIFIC GOALS for developing your skills and talents.

- Seek opportunities for learning and practice.

- Challenge yourself to improve and expand your abilities.

- Celebrate your progress and achievements.

3. Finding Fulfillment in Solitary Activities

FINDING FULFILLMENT in solitary activities involves engaging in pursuits that bring joy and satisfaction when alone. These activities help individuals develop a sense of independence and self-reliance.

Example: Maria found fulfillment in solitary activities like reading and painting. These pursuits allowed her to enjoy her own company and find satisfaction within herself.

Ideas for Solitary Activities:

- READING BOOKS OR LISTENING to audiobooks.

- Engaging in creative pursuits like painting, writing, or crafting.

- Practicing mindfulness and meditation.

- Exploring nature through hiking, birdwatching, or gardening.

4. Balancing Social and Solitary Activities

BALANCING SOCIAL AND solitary activities involves creating a healthy mix of time spent with others and time spent alone. This balance helps individuals maintain their independence while enjoying social connections.

Example: Kevin balanced his social and solitary activities by joining a photography club and also dedicating time to pursue photography alone. This balance allowed him to enjoy social interactions and personal reflection.

Strategies for Balancing Social and Solitary Activities:

- Schedule regular time for social activities with friends and family.

- Set aside dedicated time for solitary pursuits.

- Be mindful of your energy levels and adjust your activities accordingly.

- Reflect on your needs and preferences to create a balanced schedule.

5. Integrating Hobbies into Daily Life

INTEGRATING HOBBIES into daily life involves making time for activities that bring joy and satisfaction. This practice enhances overall well-being and provides a sense of fulfillment.

Example: Lisa integrated her love for music into her daily life by playing the guitar each evening. This routine brought her joy and relaxation, enhancing her overall well-being.

Tips for Integrating Hobbies into Daily Life:

- SET ASIDE SPECIFIC times each day or week for your hobbies.

- Create a dedicated space for your activities.

- Incorporate small moments of joy into your daily routine.

- Prioritize your hobbies and make them a regular part of your life.

Balancing Autonomy and Intimacy

BALANCING AUTONOMY and intimacy involves maintaining a sense of independence while fostering deep, meaningful connections with others. This balance is essential for healthy, fulfilling relationships.

1. Understanding the Need for Balance

BALANCING AUTONOMY and intimacy involves recognizing the importance of both independence and connection in relationships. Each individual's needs for autonomy and intimacy may vary, and finding the right balance is key to a healthy dynamic.

Example: John and Emily understood the importance of balancing their need for personal space with their desire for connection. They communicated openly about their needs and worked together to find a balance that worked for both of them.

Benefits of Balancing Autonomy and Intimacy:

- ENHANCED PERSONAL growth and self-development.

- Stronger, more resilient relationships.

- Greater satisfaction and fulfillment in both personal and relational aspects of life.

- Reduced feelings of resentment and dependency.

2. Communicating Needs and Boundaries

COMMUNICATING NEEDS and boundaries is essential for balancing autonomy and intimacy. Open and honest communication helps partners understand each other's needs and find ways to support each other's independence and connection.

Example: Lisa communicated her need for alone time to Kevin, explaining how it helped her recharge and feel more connected when they spent time together. Kevin respected her need and supported her in taking time for herself.

Tips for Communicating Needs and Boundaries:

- USE "I" STATEMENTS to express your needs and feelings (e.g., "I need some time alone to recharge").

- Be clear and specific about your boundaries and why they are important.

- Listen actively to your partner's needs and perspectives.

- Negotiate and find compromises that honor both partners' needs.

3. Supporting Each Other's Independence

SUPPORTING EACH OTHER'S independence involves encouraging and respecting each other's pursuits and personal growth. This support fosters mutual respect and strengthens the relationship.

Example: Mark supported Jane's pursuit of a new hobby by encouraging her to join a local club and dedicating time to help her practice. Jane, in turn, supported Mark's goals and celebrated his achievements.

Ways to Support Each Other's Independence:

- ENCOURAGE YOUR PARTNER to pursue their interests and goals.

- Celebrate their achievements and progress.

- Respect their need for personal space and time.

- Offer support and encouragement without being intrusive.

4. Nurturing Emotional Intimacy

NURTURING EMOTIONAL intimacy involves creating a safe and supportive environment for sharing thoughts, feelings, and experiences. Emotional intimacy fosters deep connection and trust in relationships.

Example: Maria and her partner nurtured emotional intimacy by setting aside regular time for deep conversations. They shared their fears, dreams, and vulnerabilities, strengthening their bond.

Steps to Nurture Emotional Intimacy:

- SCHEDULE REGULAR TIME for meaningful conversations.

- Share your thoughts, feelings, and experiences openly.

- Practice active listening and empathy.

- Create a safe and supportive environment for sharing.

5. Finding Balance in Shared Activities

FINDING BALANCE IN shared activities involves engaging in activities that both partners enjoy while also respecting each other's need for independence. This balance fosters connection and mutual enjoyment.

Example: John and Emily found balance in shared activities by planning regular date nights and weekend getaways while also pursuing their individual interests. This approach allowed them to enjoy quality time together and maintain their independence.

Tips for Finding Balance in Shared Activities:

- PLAN REGULAR ACTIVITIES that both partners enjoy.

- Schedule time for individual pursuits and respect each other's personal time.

- Be open to trying new activities together.

- Reflect on what activities bring joy and fulfillment to both partners.

6. Practicing Flexibility and Adaptability

PRACTICING FLEXIBILITY and adaptability involves being open to change and willing to adjust as needed. Relationships evolve, and maintaining a healthy balance of autonomy and intimacy requires ongoing effort and adaptation.

Example: Kevin and Lisa practiced flexibility by adjusting their routines and plans to accommodate each other's changing needs. They communicated openly and made compromises to ensure both partners felt supported and valued.

Strategies for Practicing Flexibility and Adaptability:

- Be open to discussing and adjusting your needs and boundaries.

- Recognize that relationships evolve and require ongoing effort.

- Practice patience and understanding during periods of change.

- Celebrate your ability to adapt and grow together.

7. Cultivating Mutual Respect

CULTIVATING MUTUAL respect involves valuing each other's perspectives, needs, and individuality. Respect is the foundation of a healthy balance between autonomy and intimacy.

Example: Mark and Jane cultivated mutual respect by valuing each other's opinions and supporting each other's personal growth. This respect strengthened their relationship and allowed them to maintain a healthy balance.

Ways to Cultivate Mutual Respect:

- ACKNOWLEDGE AND APPRECIATE each other's unique qualities and strengths.

- Listen actively and validate each other's feelings and perspectives.

- Support each other's goals and aspirations.

- Respect each other's boundaries and personal space.

8. Building a Strong Foundation of Trust

BUILDING A STRONG FOUNDATION of trust involves being consistent, reliable, and honest. Trust is essential for balancing autonomy and intimacy, as it allows partners to feel secure and supported.

Example: Lisa and Kevin built a strong foundation of trust by being open and honest with each other. They communicated their needs and boundaries clearly and followed through on their commitments, reinforcing their trust.

Steps to Build a Strong Foundation of Trust:

- COMMUNICATE OPENLY and honestly about your thoughts, feelings, and needs.

- Follow through on promises and commitments.

- Be consistent and reliable in your actions and behavior.

- Address issues and concerns directly and constructively.

Conclusion

Embracing independence is essential for personal well-being and healthy relationships. By understanding the importance of self-reliance and independence, cultivating hobbies and interests outside of relationships, and balancing autonomy and intimacy, individuals can develop a fulfilling and balanced life. The journey to embracing independence and building healthy relationships may be challenging, but with dedication and effort, it is possible to break free from codependent patterns and create a life filled with personal growth, meaningful connections, and mutual respect.

Chapter 10: Seeking Professional Help

Seeking professional help is a crucial step in overcoming codependency and developing healthier relationships and a stronger sense of self. This chapter explores when and how to seek therapy, types of therapy effective for codependency, and what to expect when working with a therapist.

When and How to Seek Therapy

RECOGNIZING THE NEED for professional help and taking the steps to seek therapy can be challenging yet transformative. Understanding when and how to seek therapy can provide clarity and encourage individuals to take this important step.

1. Recognizing the Need for Therapy

RECOGNIZING THE NEED for therapy involves acknowledging the signs and symptoms that indicate professional help is necessary. These signs can include emotional distress, difficulty maintaining healthy relationships, and an inability to manage daily life effectively.

Example: Jane realized she needed therapy when she found herself constantly anxious and unable to set boundaries in her relationships. Her emotional distress and difficulty managing her relationships indicated that professional help was necessary.

Signs that Indicate the Need for Therapy:

- PERSISTENT FEELINGS of sadness, anxiety, or hopelessness.

- Difficulty maintaining healthy relationships and setting boundaries.

- Emotional distress that interferes with daily functioning.

- Reliance on unhealthy coping mechanisms, such as substance abuse.

- Difficulty managing stress and emotions.

- Feeling stuck or unable to make positive changes in life.

2. Overcoming Barriers to Seeking Therapy

OVERCOMING BARRIERS to seeking therapy involves addressing common concerns and misconceptions that may prevent individuals from seeking help. These barriers can include stigma, fear, and financial constraints.

Example: Mark was hesitant to seek therapy due to the stigma associated with mental health treatment. By educating himself about the benefits of therapy and seeking support from trusted friends, he was able to overcome his fear and take the step towards seeking help.

Common Barriers and Ways to Overcome Them:

- STIGMA: EDUCATE YOURSELF about the benefits of therapy and seek support from trusted friends and family. Remember that seeking help is a sign of strength and self-awareness.

- Fear: Acknowledge your fears and concerns about therapy. Consider discussing them with a mental health professional during an initial consultation.

- Financial Constraints: Explore options for affordable therapy, such as sliding-scale fees, community mental health centers, and online therapy platforms. Check if your insurance covers mental health services.

3. Finding the Right Therapist

FINDING THE RIGHT THERAPIST involves researching and identifying professionals who specialize in codependency and related issues. It's important to find a therapist with whom you feel comfortable and confident.

Example: Maria found the right therapist by researching online and seeking recommendations from friends. She scheduled initial consultations with a few therapists to find the one who was the best fit for her needs.

Steps to Find the Right Therapist:

- RESEARCH: LOOK FOR therapists who specialize in codependency, relationships, and mental health issues. Use online directories, professional organizations, and recommendations from trusted sources.

- Initial Consultations: Schedule initial consultations with potential therapists to discuss your concerns and assess their approach and compatibility.

- Ask Questions: Inquire about the therapist's experience, qualifications, and treatment approach. Ask about their experience with codependency and their methods for addressing it.

- Trust Your Instincts: Choose a therapist with whom you feel comfortable and confident. Trust your instincts and select someone who respects your needs and goals.

4. Preparing for Therapy

PREPARING FOR THERAPY involves setting goals, gathering relevant information, and approaching the process with an open mind. Being prepared can enhance the effectiveness of therapy and help you achieve your desired outcomes.

Example: Kevin prepared for therapy by reflecting on his goals and concerns. He made a list of issues he wanted to address and approached the process with an open mind, ready to engage in the therapeutic journey.

Tips for Preparing for Therapy:

- SET GOALS: REFLECT on what you hope to achieve through therapy. Consider specific issues you want to address and the outcomes you desire.

- Gather Information: Write down relevant information about your history, experiences, and concerns. This can help provide context and facilitate discussions with your therapist.

- Be Open: Approach therapy with an open mind and a willingness to engage in the process. Be prepared to explore difficult emotions and experiences.

- Stay Committed: Therapy is a journey that requires commitment and effort. Be prepared to invest time and energy into the process.

Types of Therapy Effective for Codependency

VARIOUS TYPES OF THERAPY can be effective in addressing codependency and promoting healthier relationship patterns. Understanding these therapeutic approaches can help individuals find the right treatment for their needs.

1. Cognitive-Behavioral Therapy (CBT)

COGNITIVE-BEHAVIORAL Therapy (CBT) is a widely used and effective approach for treating codependency. CBT focuses on identifying and changing negative thought patterns and behaviors.

Example: Jane benefited from CBT by learning to recognize her negative thought patterns and replace them with healthier, more positive thoughts. This helped her develop healthier behaviors and improve her self-esteem.

Key Components of CBT:

- IDENTIFYING NEGATIVE Thoughts: Recognizing and challenging negative thought patterns that contribute to codependent behaviors.

- Behavioral Changes: Developing healthier behaviors and coping strategies to replace codependent actions.

- Skill Building: Learning skills for effective communication, emotional regulation, and problem-solving.

- Goal Setting: Setting specific, achievable goals for personal growth and relationship improvement.

2. Dialectical Behavior Therapy (DBT)

DIALECTICAL BEHAVIOR Therapy (DBT) is an evidence-based approach that combines cognitive-behavioral techniques with mindfulness practices. DBT is effective for individuals struggling with codependency, particularly those with intense emotions and difficulty regulating them.

Example: Mark found DBT helpful in managing his intense emotions and developing healthier relationship patterns. The mindfulness practices in DBT helped him stay present and respond to situations more effectively.

Key Components of DBT:

- MINDFULNESS: PRACTICING mindfulness to stay present and aware of thoughts and emotions without judgment.

- Distress Tolerance: Developing skills to manage and tolerate distressing emotions and situations.

- Emotion Regulation: Learning strategies to regulate intense emotions and reduce emotional reactivity.

- Interpersonal Effectiveness: Building skills for effective communication, boundary-setting, and relationship management.

3. Family Therapy

FAMILY THERAPY INVOLVES working with multiple family members to address dysfunctional dynamics and improve communication and relationships. Family therapy can be particularly effective for codependency that has roots in family dynamics.

Example: Maria and her family participated in family therapy to address long-standing patterns of codependency and improve their communication.

The therapy sessions helped them develop healthier dynamics and support each other's growth.

Key Components of Family Therapy:

- UNDERSTANDING FAMILY Dynamics: Exploring how family dynamics contribute to codependent behaviors and addressing these patterns.

- Improving Communication: Developing effective communication skills to enhance understanding and reduce conflicts.

- Setting Boundaries: Learning to set and respect boundaries within the family to promote healthier relationships.

- Supporting Individual Growth: Encouraging each family member's personal growth and independence.

4. Group Therapy

GROUP THERAPY INVOLVES participating in therapy sessions with a group of individuals who share similar experiences and challenges. Group therapy can provide valuable support, validation, and insights for individuals struggling with codependency.

Example: Kevin found group therapy helpful in connecting with others who faced similar challenges. Sharing experiences and learning from others provided him with valuable support and insights.

Key Components of Group Therapy:

- SHARED EXPERIENCES: Connecting with others who have similar experiences and challenges.

- Support and Validation: Receiving support and validation from group members.

- Learning from Others: Gaining insights and strategies from others' experiences.

- Building Relationships: Developing healthy relationships within the group setting.

5. Psychodynamic Therapy

PSYCHODYNAMIC THERAPY focuses on exploring unconscious thoughts and emotions that influence behavior. This approach can help individuals understand the underlying causes of their codependency and develop healthier patterns.

Example: Lisa benefited from psychodynamic therapy by exploring her past experiences and understanding how they influenced her codependent behaviors. This insight helped her develop healthier relationships.

Key Components of Psychodynamic Therapy:

- EXPLORING UNCONSCIOUS Thoughts: Uncovering and understanding unconscious thoughts and emotions that drive behavior.

- Understanding Past Experiences: Exploring past experiences and their impact on current behavior and relationships.

- Developing Insight: Gaining insight into the underlying causes of codependency and developing healthier patterns.

- Building Self-Awareness: Increasing self-awareness and understanding of one's thoughts, emotions, and behaviors.

6. Trauma-Informed Therapy

TRAUMA-INFORMED THERAPY focuses on understanding and healing the impact of past trauma on current behavior. This approach can be particularly effective for individuals whose codependency is rooted in traumatic experiences.

Example: Tom found trauma-informed therapy helpful in addressing the impact of past trauma on his codependent behaviors. The therapy sessions helped him heal and develop healthier coping strategies.

Key Components of Trauma-Informed Therapy:

- UNDERSTANDING TRAUMA: Exploring the impact of past trauma on current behavior and relationships.

- Developing Coping Strategies: Learning healthy coping strategies to manage the effects of trauma.

- Healing and Recovery: Focusing on healing and recovery from traumatic experiences.

- Building Resilience: Developing resilience and strength to cope with future challenges.

7. Integrative Therapy

INTEGRATIVE THERAPY combines elements from various therapeutic approaches to create a personalized treatment plan. This approach can be tailored to the individual's unique needs and preferences.

Example: Maria's therapist used an integrative approach, combining CBT, mindfulness, and trauma-informed techniques to address her codependency. This personalized approach helped her achieve her goals and develop healthier behaviors.

Key Components of Integrative Therapy:

- PERSONALIZED TREATMENT: Creating a treatment plan tailored to the individual's unique needs and preferences.

- Combining Approaches: Integrating techniques from various therapeutic approaches to address different aspects of codependency.

- Flexibility: Adapting the treatment plan as needed to ensure it remains effective.

- Holistic Focus: Addressing the individual's physical, emotional, and mental well-being.

Working with a Therapist: What to Expect

WORKING WITH A THERAPIST involves building a therapeutic relationship, engaging in the therapeutic process, and achieving personal growth and healing. Understanding what to expect can help individuals feel more comfortable and confident in seeking therapy.

1. Building a Therapeutic Relationship

THE THERAPEUTIC RELATIONSHIP is the foundation of effective therapy. It involves building trust, rapport, and collaboration between the therapist and the client.

Example: Jane developed a strong therapeutic relationship with her therapist by being open and honest about her experiences. Her therapist provided a supportive and non-judgmental environment, helping her feel comfortable and understood.

Steps to Build a Therapeutic Relationship:

- OPEN COMMUNICATION: Communicate openly and honestly with your therapist about your thoughts, feelings, and experiences.

- Trust and Rapport: Build trust and rapport by being consistent and reliable in your therapy sessions.

- Collaboration: Collaborate with your therapist to set goals and develop a treatment plan that aligns with your needs and preferences.

- Feedback: Provide feedback to your therapist about what is working and what isn't. This helps tailor the therapy to your needs.

2. Engaging in the Therapeutic Process

ENGAGING IN THE THERAPEUTIC process involves actively participating in therapy sessions, completing assignments, and applying what you learn to your daily life.

Example: Mark engaged in the therapeutic process by actively participating in sessions, completing homework assignments, and applying the skills he learned to his relationships. This active engagement helped him achieve his therapy goals.

Tips for Engaging in the Therapeutic Process:

- ACTIVE PARTICIPATION: Participate actively in therapy sessions by sharing your thoughts and experiences and asking questions.

- Homework Assignments: Complete any homework assignments or exercises provided by your therapist.

- Practice Skills: Practice the skills and techniques you learn in therapy in your daily life.

- Reflection: Reflect on your progress and experiences to gain insight and make adjustments as needed.

3. Setting and Achieving Goals

SETTING AND ACHIEVING goals is a key component of therapy. Goals provide direction and motivation, helping you focus on specific areas for improvement and measure your progress.

Example: Maria set specific goals for her therapy, such as developing healthier boundaries and improving her self-esteem. Working towards these goals provided direction and motivation for her therapeutic journey.

Steps to Set and Achieve Therapy Goals:

- IDENTIFY AREAS FOR Improvement: Reflect on the areas of your life and relationships that you want to improve.

- Set Specific Goals: Set specific, measurable, achievable, relevant, and time-bound (SMART) goals.

- Develop a Plan: Collaborate with your therapist to develop a plan for achieving your goals.

- Track Progress: Regularly track your progress towards your goals and make adjustments as needed.

- Celebrate Achievements: Celebrate your achievements and progress to stay motivated and reinforce positive changes.

4. Addressing Challenges and Setbacks

ADDRESSING CHALLENGES and setbacks is an important part of the therapeutic process. Therapy is a journey that may involve ups and downs, and it's important to approach challenges with resilience and perseverance.

Example: Kevin faced challenges and setbacks during his therapy, such as difficulty setting boundaries and managing his emotions. By addressing these challenges with his therapist, he developed resilience and learned valuable coping strategies.

Tips for Addressing Challenges and Setbacks:

- STAY COMMITTED: STAY committed to the therapeutic process, even when facing challenges and setbacks.

- Seek Support: Discuss challenges and setbacks with your therapist and seek their support and guidance.

- Learn from Experiences: Reflect on challenges and setbacks to learn valuable lessons and develop new strategies.

- Practice Self-Compassion: Be kind and compassionate to yourself during difficult times and recognize that setbacks are a natural part of the therapeutic journey.

5. Measuring Progress and Adjusting Treatment

MEASURING PROGRESS and adjusting treatment involves regularly assessing your progress towards your goals and making adjustments to your treatment plan as needed. This ensures that therapy remains effective and aligned with your needs.

Example: Lisa and her therapist regularly assessed her progress towards her goals. When they identified areas where progress was slower, they made adjustments to the treatment plan to address these challenges more effectively.

Steps to Measure Progress and Adjust Treatment:

- REGULAR ASSESSMENTS: Regularly assess your progress towards your therapy goals with your therapist.

- Identify Areas for Improvement: Identify areas where progress is slower or where additional support is needed.

- Adjust Treatment Plan: Collaborate with your therapist to make adjustments to your treatment plan as needed.

- Celebrate Successes: Celebrate your successes and progress to stay motivated and reinforce positive changes.

6. Transitioning Out of Therapy

TRANSITIONING OUT OF therapy involves preparing for the end of therapy and developing a plan for maintaining your progress and well-being. This transition should be done gradually and with the support of your therapist.

Example: Tom and his therapist planned his transition out of therapy by developing a maintenance plan and discussing strategies for continuing his progress. This preparation helped him feel confident and supported as he transitioned out of therapy.

Tips for Transitioning Out of Therapy:

- GRADUAL TRANSITION: Plan a gradual transition out of therapy with the support of your therapist.

- Maintenance Plan: Develop a maintenance plan to continue your progress and well-being after therapy.

- Ongoing Support: Identify ongoing sources of support, such as support groups, friends, and family.

- Regular Check-Ins: Schedule regular check-ins with your therapist or another mental health professional to monitor your progress and address any challenges.

Conclusion

Seeking professional help is a crucial step in overcoming codependency and developing healthier relationships and a stronger sense of self. By recognizing when and how to seek therapy, understanding the types of therapy effective for codependency, and knowing what to expect when working with a therapist, individuals can embark on a transformative journey of personal growth and healing. The therapeutic process may be challenging, but with dedication and effort, it is possible to break free from codependent patterns and create a fulfilling, balanced life filled with meaningful connections and personal fulfillment.

Chapter 11: Supporting a Loved One with Codependency

Supporting a loved one with codependency can be challenging and emotionally taxing. It requires a delicate balance of providing support without enabling unhealthy behaviors, recognizing the signs of codependency, and encouraging professional help and self-care. This chapter explores how to recognize codependency in others, how to offer support effectively, and how to promote professional help and self-care.

Recognizing Codependency in Others

RECOGNIZING CODEPENDENCY in a loved one is the first step in providing effective support. Codependency often manifests through specific behaviors and emotional patterns that can be identified with careful observation.

1. Common Signs of Codependency

CODEPENDENCY CAN BE identified through a range of emotional, behavioral, and psychological signs. Understanding these signs can help you recognize codependency in a loved one and take appropriate steps to support them.

Emotional Signs:

- LOW SELF-ESTEEM: INDIVIDUALS with codependency often struggle with feelings of inadequacy and unworthiness. They may constantly seek validation from others and doubt their abilities.

- Anxiety and Worry: A pervasive sense of anxiety and worry, especially about others' well-being, is common. Codependent individuals often feel responsible for others' happiness and success.

- Guilt and Shame: Feelings of guilt and shame are prevalent, particularly when setting boundaries or prioritizing their own needs. They may feel they are being selfish or neglectful.

- Emotional Numbness: To cope with overwhelming emotions, codependent individuals may detach and become emotionally numb. They might have difficulty identifying and expressing their own feelings.

- Resentment: Despite their self-sacrificing behavior, codependent individuals often feel resentment towards others for not reciprocating or appreciating their efforts. This can lead to feelings of anger and bitterness.

Behavioral Signs:

- EXCESSIVE CARETAKING: Codependent individuals often go to great lengths to care for others, even at their own expense. They might feel responsible for other people's happiness and well-being, neglecting their own needs in the process.

- People-Pleasing: A strong desire to be liked and accepted can drive codependent behavior. Individuals may find it hard to say no and often agree to things they do not want to do to avoid conflict or rejection.

- Control Issues: Despite often appearing passive, codependent individuals may exert a great deal of control over others to feel safe and secure. This control can manifest through manipulation, guilt-tripping, or other indirect means.

- Poor Boundaries: Boundaries are essential for healthy relationships, but codependent individuals often struggle with them. They might have blurred or non-existent boundaries, making it hard to separate their own needs and feelings from those of others.

- Dependency: Codependent individuals may rely heavily on others for their sense of self-worth and identity. This dependency can make it difficult for them to function independently.

Example: Jane's partner, Mark, exhibits several signs of codependency. He constantly worries about Jane's well-being, even when there is no cause for concern. Mark often sacrifices his own needs to take care of Jane, feels guilty when he tries to set boundaries, and relies on Jane's approval to feel good about himself.

2. Understanding the Impact of Codependency on Relationships

CODEPENDENCY CAN SIGNIFICANTLY impact relationships, creating imbalances and unhealthy dynamics. Recognizing these impacts can help you understand the challenges your loved one faces and provide more effective support.

Imbalances in Caretaking: In codependent relationships, one person often assumes the role of caretaker, while the other becomes dependent. This imbalance can lead to resentment, frustration, and burnout.

Example: Maria constantly takes care of her partner, John, who struggles with anxiety. While she genuinely wants to help, the imbalance in their relationship leaves her feeling exhausted and unappreciated.

Lack of Boundaries: Codependent relationships often lack healthy boundaries, leading to enmeshment and a loss of individuality. This can stifle personal growth and create a sense of suffocation.

Example: Kevin and Lisa struggle with setting boundaries in their relationship. Kevin feels overwhelmed by Lisa's constant need for attention, while Lisa feels neglected when Kevin tries to take time for himself.

Emotional Dependency: Codependent individuals often rely on their partners for emotional support and validation, leading to a lack of self-sufficiency and an unhealthy level of dependency.

Example: Tom depends on his partner, Emily, for emotional support. He feels unable to cope with his emotions without her reassurance, creating a dynamic where Emily feels pressured to be constantly available.

3. Observing Behavioral Patterns

OBSERVING BEHAVIORAL patterns can help you identify codependency in a loved one. Pay attention to how they interact with others, manage their responsibilities, and respond to stress.

Over-Involvement in Others' Lives: Codependent individuals often become overly involved in others' lives, taking on responsibilities that are not their own and neglecting their needs.

Example: Jane's friend, Sarah, is constantly involved in her family members' problems, often at the expense of her well-being. Sarah neglects her own needs to ensure her family is happy and taken care of.

Difficulty Saying No: Codependent individuals often struggle to say no, even when it is detrimental to their well-being. They may agree to things they do not want to do to avoid conflict or rejection.

Example: Mark frequently agrees to help his colleagues with their work, even when he is overwhelmed with his own tasks. He finds it hard to say no and fears disappointing others.

Seeking Validation: Codependent individuals often seek validation from others to feel good about themselves. They may rely on external approval to boost their self-esteem.

Example: Maria constantly seeks reassurance from her partner and friends. She doubts her abilities and decisions unless they are validated by others.

Enabling Unhealthy Behaviors: Codependent individuals may enable unhealthy behaviors in others, such as substance abuse or irresponsibility, in an attempt to maintain control or avoid conflict.

Example: Kevin enables his brother's drinking problem by making excuses for him and covering up his mistakes. He fears that addressing the issue will lead to conflict and rejection.

Providing Support Without Enabling

PROVIDING SUPPORT TO a loved one with codependency requires a delicate balance. It is essential to offer help and encouragement without enabling unhealthy behaviors or perpetuating codependent patterns.

1. Setting Healthy Boundaries

SETTING HEALTHY BOUNDARIES is crucial for providing support without enabling. Boundaries protect your well-being and ensure that your support is constructive and sustainable.

Example: Jane sets boundaries with Mark by clearly communicating her limits. She explains that while she is there to support him, she also needs time for herself to recharge and maintain her well-being.

Tips for Setting Healthy Boundaries:

- COMMUNICATE CLEARLY: Express your boundaries clearly and respectfully. Use "I" statements to convey your needs and limits (e.g., "I need some time for myself each evening to recharge").

- Be Consistent: Consistently enforce your boundaries to ensure they are respected. Follow through with any consequences if your boundaries are violated.

- Practice Self-Care: Prioritize your self-care and well-being. Ensure that your support for your loved one does not come at the expense of your needs.

- Seek Support: Seek support from friends, family, or a therapist to help you navigate the challenges of setting and maintaining boundaries.

2. Encouraging Independence

ENCOURAGING INDEPENDENCE involves supporting your loved one in developing self-reliance and personal growth. This helps them build self-esteem and reduce their reliance on others for validation and support.

Example: Mark encourages Jane to pursue her interests and hobbies independently. He supports her in setting personal goals and celebrates her achievements, helping her build confidence and independence.

Ways to Encourage Independence:

- Support Personal Goals: Encourage your loved one to set and pursue personal goals. Celebrate their achievements and progress.

- Promote Self-Care: Encourage them to prioritize self-care and engage in activities that nurture their well-being.

- Foster Problem-Solving Skills: Support them in developing problem-solving skills and making decisions independently.

- Encourage Hobbies and Interests: Encourage them to explore and pursue hobbies and interests outside of their relationships.

3. Providing Emotional Support

PROVIDING EMOTIONAL support involves offering empathy, understanding, and encouragement without enabling codependent behaviors. Emotional support helps your loved one feel valued and understood.

Example: Maria provides emotional support to John by listening to his concerns and offering empathy. She validates his feelings without taking on the responsibility for solving his problems.

Tips for Providing Emotional Support:

- LISTEN ACTIVELY: PRACTICE active listening by giving your full attention and reflecting back what you have heard.

- Validate Feelings: Acknowledge and validate your loved one's feelings and experiences without judgment.

- Offer Encouragement: Encourage them to express their emotions and seek healthy coping strategies.

- Avoid Taking Over: Offer support and guidance without taking over or solving their problems for them.

4. Promoting Healthy Communication

PROMOTING HEALTHY COMMUNICATION involves fostering open, honest, and respectful dialogue. Effective communication helps build trust and understanding, reducing the risk of enabling codependent behaviors.

Example: Kevin promotes healthy communication with Lisa by encouraging open and honest conversations. They discuss their needs and concerns respectfully, ensuring that both partners feel heard and valued.

Tips for Promoting Healthy Communication:

- USE "I" STATEMENTS: Express your feelings and needs using "I" statements (e.g., "I feel concerned when...").

- Listen Without Interrupting: Allow your loved one to express themselves without interrupting or judging.

- Clarify and Reflect: Reflect back what you have heard to ensure understanding and clarify any misunderstandings.

- Stay Calm and Respectful: Maintain a calm and respectful tone, even during difficult conversations.

5. Avoiding Enabling Behaviors

AVOIDING ENABLING BEHAVIORS involves recognizing and addressing actions that perpetuate codependency. It is essential to provide support that empowers your loved one rather than reinforcing their dependency.

Example: Tom avoids enabling Emily's emotional dependency by encouraging her to develop healthy coping strategies. He supports her in seeking therapy and engaging in activities that promote self-reliance.

Ways to Avoid Enabling Behaviors:

- ENCOURAGE ACCOUNTABILITY: Encourage your loved one to take responsibility for their actions and decisions.

- Promote Problem-Solving: Support them in developing problem-solving skills and addressing their challenges independently.

- Set Boundaries: Set and enforce healthy boundaries to prevent over-involvement and burnout.

- Foster Self-Reliance: Encourage them to develop self-reliance and seek help from professionals when needed.

Encouraging Professional Help and Self-Care

ENCOURAGING PROFESSIONAL help and self-care is essential for supporting a loved one with codependency. Professional help provides the tools and guidance needed for recovery, while self-care promotes overall well-being.

1. Discussing the Benefits of Therapy

DISCUSSING THE BENEFITS of therapy can help your loved one understand the value of seeking professional help. Therapy provides a safe space to explore their experiences, develop healthier behaviors, and build self-esteem.

Example: Jane discusses the benefits of therapy with Mark, explaining how it can help him understand his codependent behaviors and develop healthier relationship patterns. She emphasizes that therapy is a supportive and non-judgmental environment.

Tips for Discussing the Benefits of Therapy:

- BE SUPPORTIVE: APPROACH the conversation with empathy and understanding. Emphasize that seeking therapy is a sign of strength and self-awareness.

- Share Information: Provide information about the benefits of therapy, including how it can help address codependency and improve well-being.

- Encourage an Open Mind: Encourage your loved one to approach therapy with an open mind and a willingness to engage in the process.

- Offer to Help: Offer to help them find a therapist or accompany them to their first appointment if they feel nervous.

2. Finding the Right Therapist

FINDING THE RIGHT THERAPIST involves researching professionals who specialize in codependency and related issues. A good therapist provides the support and guidance needed for recovery.

Example: Mark helps Jane find a therapist by researching professionals who specialize in codependency. He provides her with a list of potential therapists and offers to accompany her to her first appointment.

Steps to Find the Right Therapist:

- Research: Look for therapists who specialize in codependency, relationships, and mental health issues. Use online directories, professional organizations, and recommendations from trusted sources.

- Initial Consultations: Schedule initial consultations with potential therapists to discuss your loved one's concerns and assess their approach and compatibility.

- Ask Questions: Inquire about the therapist's experience, qualifications, and treatment approach. Ask about their experience with codependency and their methods for addressing it.

- Trust Instincts: Encourage your loved one to choose a therapist with whom they feel comfortable and confident. Trust their instincts and select someone who respects their needs and goals.

3. Supporting the Therapy Process

SUPPORTING THE THERAPY process involves encouraging your loved one to engage actively in therapy and providing ongoing support. This support helps them stay committed and motivated.

Example: Maria supports John's therapy process by encouraging him to attend his sessions regularly and discussing his progress. She provides a listening ear and celebrates his achievements, reinforcing his commitment to therapy.

Tips for Supporting the Therapy Process:

- ENCOURAGE REGULAR Attendance Encourage your loved one to attend therapy sessions regularly and stay committed to the process.

- Discuss Progress: Discuss their progress and any challenges they face. Offer empathy and understanding without judgment.

- Celebrate Achievements: Celebrate their achievements and progress to reinforce positive changes.

- Provide a Supportive Environment: Create a supportive environment that encourages open communication and emotional expression.

4. Promoting Self-Care

PROMOTING SELF-CARE involves encouraging your loved one to prioritize their well-being and engage in activities that nurture their physical, emotional, and mental health.

Example: Kevin promotes self-care by encouraging Lisa to engage in activities that bring her joy and relaxation. He supports her in setting aside time for self-care and emphasizes its importance for overall well-being.

Ways to Promote Self-Care:

- ENCOURAGE REGULAR Self-Care: Encourage your loved one to engage in regular self-care activities, such as exercise, relaxation, and hobbies.

- Support Healthy Habits: Support them in developing healthy habits, such as eating well, getting enough sleep, and managing stress.

- Model Self-Care: Model self-care by prioritizing your well-being and engaging in self-care activities yourself.

- Provide Resources: Provide resources and information about self-care practices and activities that can benefit their well-being.

5. Building a Support Network

BUILDING A SUPPORT network involves encouraging your loved one to seek support from friends, family, and support groups. A strong support network provides validation, encouragement, and a sense of belonging.

Example: Tom encourages Emily to join a support group for individuals struggling with codependency. He also helps her connect with friends and family who can provide additional support.

Tips for Building a Support Network:

- ENCOURAGE SUPPORT Groups: Encourage your loved one to join support groups, such as Codependents Anonymous, where they can connect with others facing similar challenges.

- Foster Connections: Help them foster connections with friends and family who provide positive and supportive influences.

- Seek Professional Support: Encourage them to seek professional support from therapists, counselors, and other mental health professionals.

- Be Part of Their Support Network: Offer your support and be part of their support network by providing empathy, understanding, and encouragement.

6. Encouraging Healthy Lifestyle Changes

ENCOURAGING HEALTHY lifestyle changes involves supporting your loved one in developing habits that promote overall well-being. Healthy lifestyle changes can reduce stress, improve mood, and enhance physical health.

Example: Maria encourages John to make healthy lifestyle changes, such as exercising regularly, eating a balanced diet, and getting enough sleep. She supports him in making these changes by joining him in healthy activities and providing encouragement.

Tips for Encouraging Healthy Lifestyle Changes:

- PROMOTE PHYSICAL ACTIVITY: Encourage regular physical activity, such as walking, jogging, or yoga, to improve physical and mental health.

- Support Healthy Eating: Support your loved one in developing healthy eating habits, such as incorporating more fruits and vegetables into their diet.

- Encourage Adequate Sleep: Emphasize the importance of getting enough sleep and establishing a regular sleep routine.

- Manage Stress: Encourage stress management techniques, such as mindfulness, meditation, and relaxation exercises.

7. Celebrating Progress and Success

CELEBRATING PROGRESS and success involves acknowledging and celebrating your loved one's achievements and milestones. Positive reinforcement helps reinforce healthy behaviors and motivates continued progress.

Example: Kevin celebrates Lisa's progress by acknowledging her achievements and milestones. He expresses pride in her efforts and provides positive reinforcement, motivating her to continue her journey.

Ways to Celebrate Progress and Success:

- ACKNOWLEDGE ACHIEVEMENTS: Acknowledge and celebrate your loved one's achievements and milestones, no matter how small.

- Express Pride and Encouragement: Express pride in their efforts and provide encouragement to continue their journey.

- Celebrate Together: Celebrate their progress together by doing something enjoyable, such as going out for a meal or planning a fun activity.

- Reflect on Growth: Reflect on their growth and progress, emphasizing how far they have come and the positive changes they have made.

Conclusion

Supporting a loved one with codependency requires recognizing the signs of codependency, providing support without enabling, and encouraging professional help and self-care. By setting healthy boundaries, promoting independence, offering emotional support, and fostering healthy communication, you can help your loved one develop healthier relationship patterns and build a stronger sense of self. Encouraging professional help and self-care is essential for their recovery and well-being. The journey to overcoming codependency is challenging, but with dedication and support, it is possible to create a fulfilling, balanced life filled with meaningful connections and personal growth.

Chapter 12: Codependency in Special Populations

Codependency can affect individuals across all demographic groups, each with its own unique challenges and strategies for coping. Understanding how codependency manifests in different populations, such as teenagers and the elderly, is crucial for providing effective support and resources. This chapter explores codependency in various demographic groups, highlights the unique challenges they face, and offers strategies and resources to support each group.

Codependency in Teenagers

Teenagers are at a developmental stage where they are forming their identities and learning about relationships. Codependency can significantly impact their emotional and psychological growth, leading to unhealthy relationship patterns that can persist into adulthood.

1. Characteristics of Codependency in Teenagers

CODEPENDENCY IN TEENAGERS often stems from family dynamics, peer relationships, and societal pressures. Recognizing the characteristics of codependency in this age group can help parents, educators, and counselors provide appropriate support.

Example: Sarah, a high school student, constantly seeks approval from her friends and family. She feels responsible for her friends' happiness and often sacrifices her own needs to please others. Her low self-esteem and fear of rejection drive her codependent behaviors.

Common Characteristics:

- EXCESSIVE CARETAKING: Teenagers may feel responsible for their peers' or family members' well-being, often at the expense of their own needs.

- People-Pleasing: A strong desire to be liked and accepted can lead to people-pleasing behaviors, where teenagers agree to things they do not want to do to avoid conflict or rejection.

- Low Self-Esteem: Teenagers with codependency often struggle with feelings of inadequacy and unworthiness. They may rely on external validation to feel good about themselves.

- Difficulty Setting Boundaries: Setting boundaries can be challenging for codependent teenagers, leading to over-involvement in others' lives and a lack of personal space.

2. Unique Challenges for Teenagers

TEENAGERS FACE UNIQUE challenges related to codependency, influenced by their developmental stage, family dynamics, and peer relationships.

Peer Pressure and Social Media: The pressure to fit in and be accepted by peers can exacerbate codependent behaviors. Social media can intensify these pressures, as teenagers seek validation through likes, comments, and followers.

Example: Mark feels pressured to conform to his friends' expectations and constantly seeks validation through social media. His desire to be liked leads to codependent behaviors, such as neglecting his own needs to please others.

Family Dynamics: Family dynamics, such as parental expectations and sibling relationships, can contribute to codependency. Teenagers may feel responsible for their parents' or siblings' happiness and well-being.

Example: Maria feels responsible for her younger siblings' well-being due to her parents' frequent absences. She takes on a caretaking role, neglecting her own needs and struggling with codependency.

Identity Formation: Teenagers are in the process of forming their identities and learning about relationships. Codependency can hinder this development, leading to a lack of self-awareness and personal growth.

Example: Kevin struggles with codependency as he tries to form his identity. He relies heavily on his friends for validation and approval, making it difficult for him to develop a strong sense of self.

3. Strategies for Supporting Teenagers

SUPPORTING TEENAGERS with codependency involves providing guidance, resources, and a supportive environment to help them develop healthier relationship patterns and build self-esteem.

Open Communication: Encourage open and honest communication about feelings, relationships, and challenges. Create a safe space for teenagers to express themselves without fear of judgment.

Example: Sarah's parents encourage her to talk about her feelings and experiences. They listen without judgment and provide guidance and support, helping her develop healthier communication skills.

Promote Self-Esteem: Support teenagers in building self-esteem through positive reinforcement, recognizing their achievements, and encouraging self-compassion.

Example: Mark's teacher recognizes his achievements in class and encourages him to pursue his interests. This positive reinforcement helps boost his self-esteem and reduces his reliance on external validation.

Set Healthy Boundaries: Teach teenagers the importance of setting and respecting boundaries in relationships. Provide guidance on how to communicate boundaries effectively and assertively.

Example: Maria's counselor helps her understand the importance of setting boundaries with her family. They work together to develop strategies for communicating her needs and limits.

Encourage Independence: Encourage teenagers to pursue their interests and goals independently. Support them in developing problem-solving skills and making decisions based on their values and priorities.

Example: Kevin's coach encourages him to pursue his passion for sports independently. This support helps Kevin build confidence and develop a sense of autonomy.

Provide Resources: Provide resources such as books, articles, and support groups that address codependency and promote healthy relationship patterns.

Example: Sarah's school counselor provides her with resources on codependency and healthy relationships. They discuss these resources together, helping Sarah gain a better understanding of her behaviors.

Codependency in the Elderly

THE ELDERLY POPULATION faces unique challenges related to codependency, influenced by factors such as aging, loss of independence, and changing family dynamics. Understanding these challenges and providing appropriate support is crucial for promoting well-being in older adults.

1. Characteristics of Codependency in the Elderly

CODEPENDENCY IN THE elderly can manifest in various ways, influenced by their life experiences, health conditions, and family relationships. Recognizing these characteristics can help caregivers and family members provide effective support.

Example: John, an elderly man, feels responsible for his adult children's happiness and well-being. He often sacrifices his own needs to support them financially and emotionally, leading to codependent behaviors.

Common Characteristics:

- Caretaking Role: The elderly may take on a caretaking role for their adult children or spouse, often at the expense of their own needs.

- Fear of Abandonment: Fear of abandonment and loneliness can drive codependent behaviors, leading the elderly to seek constant validation and reassurance from their loved ones.

- Difficulty Letting Go: The elderly may struggle with letting go of control and allowing their adult children to make independent decisions. This can lead to over-involvement and codependent behaviors.

- Low Self-Esteem: Low self-esteem and feelings of inadequacy can contribute to codependency in the elderly, making them reliant on others for validation and support.

2. Unique Challenges for the Elderly

THE ELDERLY FACE UNIQUE challenges related to codependency, influenced by factors such as aging, health conditions, and changing family dynamics.

Loss of Independence: Aging and health conditions can lead to a loss of independence, making the elderly more reliant on their loved ones for support. This dependency can exacerbate codependent behaviors.

Example: Maria, an elderly woman, struggles with codependency as she becomes more reliant on her adult children for daily support. Her fear of being a burden drives her to overextend herself to please them.

Changing Family Dynamics: Changing family dynamics, such as the loss of a spouse or the role reversal with adult children becoming caregivers, can contribute to codependency in the elderly.

Example: Kevin feels responsible for his elderly mother's well-being after his father's passing. This role reversal leads to codependent behaviors, as he struggles to balance his own needs with his caregiving responsibilities.

Social Isolation: Social isolation and loneliness can drive codependent behaviors in the elderly, leading them to seek constant validation and reassurance from their loved ones.

Example: John experiences social isolation after moving to a new community. His loneliness drives him to seek constant validation from his adult children, leading to codependent behaviors.

3. Strategies for Supporting the Elderly

SUPPORTING THE ELDERLY with codependency involves providing emotional support, promoting independence, and encouraging healthy relationships. Caregivers and family members play a crucial role in this process.

Promote Independence: Encourage the elderly to maintain their independence by supporting them in daily activities and decision-making. Provide opportunities for them to engage in hobbies and social activities.

Example: Maria's family encourages her to participate in community activities and pursue her interests. This support helps her maintain her independence and reduces her reliance on her family for validation.

Provide Emotional Support: Offer emotional support and validation without enabling codependent behaviors. Encourage open communication and create a safe space for the elderly to express their feelings.

Example: Kevin provides emotional support to his mother by listening to her concerns and offering empathy. He validates her feelings without taking on the responsibility for solving her problems.

Encourage Healthy Boundaries: Help the elderly understand the importance of setting and respecting boundaries in relationships. Provide guidance on how to communicate boundaries effectively.

Example: John's caregiver helps him set boundaries with his adult children. They work together to develop strategies for communicating his needs and limits, promoting healthier relationship dynamics.

Foster Social Connections: Encourage the elderly to build and maintain social connections through community activities, support groups, and social events. Social connections provide validation and support, reducing the reliance on family members.

Example: Maria joins a local senior center and participates in social events. These activities help her build new friendships and reduce her reliance on her family for emotional support.

Provide Resources: Provide resources such as books, articles, and support groups that address codependency and promote healthy relationship patterns.

Example: Kevin's caregiver provides him with resources on codependency and healthy relationships. They discuss these resources together, helping Kevin gain a better understanding of his behaviors.

Codependency in Other Demographic Groups

CODEPENDENCY CAN AFFECT various other demographic groups, each with its own unique challenges and strategies for coping. Understanding these challenges and providing appropriate support is essential for promoting well-being across diverse populations.

Codependency in Adults with Disabilities

ADULTS WITH DISABILITIES may face unique challenges related to codependency, influenced by factors such as dependency on caregivers, social isolation, and societal attitudes.

Example: Lisa, an adult with a physical disability, relies on her caregiver for daily support. Her fear of being a burden drives her to overextend herself to please her caregiver, leading to codependent behaviors.

Common Characteristics:

- DEPENDENCY ON CAREGIVERS: Dependency on caregivers for daily support can contribute to codependency, leading individuals to seek constant validation and reassurance.

- Social Isolation: Social isolation and limited opportunities for social interaction can exacerbate codependent behaviors.

- Low Self-Esteem: Low self-esteem and feelings of inadequacy can contribute to codependency, making individuals reliant on others for validation and support.

Strategies for Supporting Adults with Disabilities:

- Promote Independence: Encourage individuals to maintain their independence by supporting them in daily activities and decision-making. Provide opportunities for them to engage in hobbies and social activities.

- Provide Emotional Support: Offer emotional support and validation without enabling codependent behaviors. Encourage open communication and create a safe space for individuals to express their feelings.

- Encourage Healthy Boundaries: Help individuals understand the importance of setting and respecting boundaries in relationships. Provide guidance on how to communicate boundaries effectively.

- Foster Social Connections: Encourage individuals to build and maintain social connections through community activities, support groups, and social events. Social connections provide validation and support, reducing reliance on caregivers.

- Provide Resources: Provide resources such as books, articles, and support groups that address codependency and promote healthy relationship patterns.

Codependency in LGBTQ+ Individuals

LGBTQ+ INDIVIDUALS may face unique challenges related to codependency, influenced by factors such as societal attitudes, family dynamics, and experiences of discrimination.

Example: Mark, a gay man, struggles with codependency due to his fear of rejection and discrimination. He seeks constant validation from his partner and friends, leading to codependent behaviors.

Common Characteristics:

- FEAR OF REJECTION: Fear of rejection and discrimination can drive codependent behaviors, leading individuals to seek constant validation and reassurance from others.

- Family Dynamics: Family dynamics, such as lack of acceptance or support, can contribute to codependency. Individuals may feel responsible for maintaining family harmony and avoiding conflict.

- Low Self-Esteem: Low self-esteem and feelings of inadequacy can contribute to codependency, making individuals reliant on others for validation and support.

Strategies for Supporting LGBTQ+ Individuals:

- PROVIDE EMOTIONAL Support: Offer emotional support and validation without enabling codependent behaviors. Encourage open communication and create a safe space for individuals to express their feelings.

- Promote Self-Esteem: Support individuals in building self-esteem through positive reinforcement, recognizing their achievements, and encouraging self-compassion.

- Encourage Independence: Encourage individuals to pursue their interests and goals independently. Support them in developing problem-solving skills and making decisions based on their values and priorities.

- Foster Social Connections: Encourage individuals to build and maintain social connections through community activities, support groups, and social events. Social connections provide validation and support, reducing reliance on partners or family members.

- Provide Resources: Provide resources such as books, articles, and support groups that address codependency and promote healthy relationship patterns.

Codependency in Caregivers

CAREGIVERS, INCLUDING those caring for family members with chronic illnesses or disabilities, may face unique challenges related to codependency. The caregiving role can lead to over-involvement and neglect of personal needs.

Example: Sarah, a caregiver for her elderly mother, struggles with codependency as she feels responsible for her mother's well-being. She neglects her own needs and relies on her mother's approval for validation.

Common Characteristics:

- EXCESSIVE CARETAKING: Caregivers may feel responsible for their loved one's well-being, often at the expense of their own needs.

- Difficulty Setting Boundaries: Setting boundaries can be challenging for caregivers, leading to over-involvement and a lack of personal space.

- Low Self-Esteem: Low self-esteem and feelings of inadequacy can contribute to codependency, making caregivers reliant on others for validation and support.

Strategies for Supporting Caregivers:

- PROMOTE SELF-CARE: Encourage caregivers to prioritize self-care and engage in activities that nurture their well-being.

- Set Healthy Boundaries: Help caregivers understand the importance of setting and respecting boundaries in their caregiving role. Provide guidance on how to communicate boundaries effectively.

- Provide Emotional Support: Offer emotional support and validation without enabling codependent behaviors. Encourage open communication and create a safe space for caregivers to express their feelings.

- Foster Social Connections: Encourage caregivers to build and maintain social connections through community activities, support groups, and social events. Social connections provide validation and support, reducing reliance on caregiving roles.

- Provide Resources: Provide resources such as books, articles, and support groups that address codependency and promote healthy relationship patterns.

Resources and Support Systems Available

VARIOUS RESOURCES AND support systems are available to help individuals and their loved ones address codependency and develop healthier relationship patterns. These resources provide information, guidance, and support for individuals across different demographic groups.

1. Books and Articles

BOOKS AND ARTICLES on codependency provide valuable information and insights into codependent behaviors, their impact, and strategies for recovery. These resources can be helpful for individuals seeking to understand and address their codependency.

Recommended Books:

- "CODEPENDENT NO MORE: How to Stop Controlling Others and Start Caring for Yourself" by Melody Beattie

- "The New Codependency: Help and Guidance for Today's Generation" by Melody Beattie

- "Facing Codependence: What It Is, Where It Comes from, How It Sabotages Our Lives" by Pia Mellody

- "The Language of Letting Go: Daily Meditations for Codependents" by Melody Beattie

- "The Codependency Workbook: Simple Practices for Developing and Maintaining Your Independence" by Krystal Mazzola Wood

2. Support Groups

SUPPORT GROUPS, SUCH as Codependents Anonymous (CoDA), provide a safe space for individuals to share their experiences, receive support, and learn from others facing similar challenges. Support groups offer validation, encouragement, and practical strategies for recovery.

Example: Lisa joins a Codependents Anonymous group and finds it helpful to connect with others who understand her struggles. The support and encouragement she receives help her develop healthier relationship patterns.

3. Therapy and Counseling

THERAPY AND COUNSELING provide professional support and guidance for individuals struggling with codependency. Therapists can help individuals explore the underlying causes of their codependency, develop healthier behaviors, and build self-esteem.

Example: Mark seeks therapy to address his codependency and develop healthier relationship patterns. His therapist helps him understand the root causes of his behaviors and provides strategies for building self-esteem and setting boundaries.

4. Online Resources

Online resources, such as websites, forums, and webinars, provide information, support, and guidance for individuals addressing codependency. These resources offer accessibility and convenience for individuals seeking help.

Recommended Websites:

- CODEPENDENTS ANONYMOUS (CoDA): www.coda.org

- Melody Beattie's website: www.melodybeattie.com

- Psychology Today: www.psychologytoday.com

- National Institute of Mental Health (NIMH): www.nimh.nih.gov

- Mental Health America: www.mhanational.org

5. Community Programs

COMMUNITY PROGRAMS, such as workshops, seminars, and educational sessions, provide opportunities for individuals to learn about codependency and develop healthier relationship patterns. These programs often offer practical strategies and support for recovery.

Example: Sarah attends a community workshop on codependency and healthy relationships. The workshop provides valuable information and practical strategies for addressing her codependency and developing healthier behaviors.

6. Peer Support

Peer support involves connecting with individuals who have experienced similar challenges and can provide empathy, validation, and encouragement. Peer support can be found through support groups, online forums, and community programs.

Example: Kevin connects with a peer support group for caregivers. The group provides him with valuable insights, support, and encouragement, helping him navigate the challenges of caregiving and codependency.

7. Educational Resources

EDUCATIONAL RESOURCES, such as books, articles, and online courses, provide information and guidance on codependency and healthy relationships. These resources can help individuals gain a better understanding of their behaviors and develop healthier patterns.

Example: Maria enrolls in an online course on codependency and healthy relationships. The course provides her with valuable information and practical strategies for addressing her codependency and building healthier relationships.

Conclusion

Codependency can affect individuals across various demographic groups, each with its own unique challenges and strategies for coping. Understanding how codependency manifests in different populations, such as teenagers, the elderly, adults with disabilities, LGBTQ+ individuals, and caregivers, is crucial for providing effective support and resources. By recognizing the characteristics of codependency, providing appropriate support, and encouraging professional help and self-care, we can help individuals develop healthier relationship patterns and build a stronger sense of self. Various resources and support systems are available to assist individuals in their journey towards recovery and well-being, offering information, guidance, and encouragement. The journey to overcoming codependency is challenging, but with dedication, support, and the right resources, it is possible to create a fulfilling, balanced life filled with meaningful connections and personal growth.

Chapter 13: Long-Term Recovery

Long-term recovery from codependency is an ongoing journey that requires dedication, self-awareness, and continuous effort. Maintaining progress and preventing relapse, engaging in ongoing support groups and communities, and adapting to life changes and challenges are crucial components of this journey. This chapter explores these aspects in depth, providing strategies and insights for sustaining long-term recovery.

Maintaining Progress and Preventing Relapse

MAINTAINING PROGRESS and preventing relapse involves a combination of self-awareness, healthy habits, and proactive strategies. Recognizing potential triggers, staying committed to self-care, and seeking support when needed are essential for long-term recovery.

1. Recognizing and Managing Triggers

RECOGNIZING AND MANAGING triggers is crucial for preventing relapse. Triggers can be people, situations, or emotions that prompt codependent behaviors. Being aware of these triggers and developing strategies to manage them can help maintain progress.

Example: Jane identified that family gatherings often triggered her codependent behaviors, as she felt compelled to take care of everyone. By recognizing this trigger, she developed strategies to manage her reactions, such as setting boundaries and taking breaks when needed.

Steps to Recognize and Manage Triggers:

- IDENTIFY TRIGGERS: Reflect on situations, people, or emotions that prompt codependent behaviors. Keep a journal to track patterns and identify common triggers.

- Develop Coping Strategies: Create a plan for managing triggers, such as setting boundaries, practicing mindfulness, or seeking support from a trusted friend or therapist.

- Stay Mindful: Practice mindfulness to stay present and aware of your thoughts and emotions. This can help you recognize and respond to triggers more effectively.

- Practice Self-Compassion: Be kind to yourself when faced with triggers. Recognize that relapse is a natural part of the recovery process and use it as an opportunity to learn and grow.

2. Staying Committed to Self-Care

STAYING COMMITTED TO self-care is essential for maintaining progress in recovery. Regular self-care activities promote physical, emotional, and mental well-being, helping to prevent relapse and sustain healthy behaviors.

Example: Mark incorporated regular self-care activities into his routine, such as exercise, meditation, and spending time with friends. These practices helped him maintain his progress and reduce the risk of relapse.

Tips for Staying Committed to Self-Care:

- CREATE A ROUTINE: Establish a regular self-care routine that includes activities that nurture your physical, emotional, and mental well-being.

- Prioritize Self-Care: Make self-care a priority in your daily life. Set aside time for activities that bring you joy and relaxation.

- Listen to Your Body: Pay attention to your body's needs and signals. Rest when you're tired, eat when you're hungry, and seek support when you're feeling overwhelmed.

- Practice Self-Compassion: Be kind and compassionate to yourself, especially during challenging times. Recognize that self-care is essential for your well-being and recovery.

3. Setting and Reviewing Goals

SETTING AND REVIEWING goals is an important part of maintaining progress in recovery. Goals provide direction and motivation, helping you stay focused on your personal growth and development.

Example: Maria set specific goals for her recovery, such as developing healthier boundaries and improving her self-esteem. She regularly reviewed her progress and adjusted her goals as needed to stay on track.

Steps for Setting and Reviewing Goals:

- IDENTIFY AREAS FOR Improvement: Reflect on areas of your life and relationships that you want to improve. Consider your long-term vision for your recovery and well-being.

- Set Specific Goals: Set specific, measurable, achievable, relevant, and time-bound (SMART) goals that align with your vision.

- Develop a Plan: Create a plan for achieving your goals, including specific actions and steps you will take.

- Review Progress: Regularly review your progress towards your goals. Celebrate your achievements and make adjustments as needed.

- Stay Flexible: Be flexible and open to adjusting your goals as your needs and circumstances change.

4. Seeking Ongoing Support

SEEKING ONGOING SUPPORT is crucial for maintaining progress in recovery. Support from friends, family, therapists, and support groups provides validation, encouragement, and accountability.

Example: Kevin continued to attend support group meetings and therapy sessions regularly. This ongoing support helped him stay committed to his recovery and navigate challenges effectively.

Tips for Seeking Ongoing Support:

- STAY CONNECTED: STAY connected with your support network, including friends, family, therapists, and support groups. Regularly reach out for support and encouragement.

- Participate in Support Groups: Attend support group meetings regularly to connect with others who understand your experiences and provide mutual support.

- Seek Professional Help: Continue to work with a therapist or counselor to address any ongoing challenges and receive guidance and support.

- Build a Diverse Support Network: Build a diverse support network that includes different types of support, such as emotional, practical, and social.

The Role of Ongoing Support Groups and Communities

ONGOING SUPPORT GROUPS and communities play a vital role in long-term recovery from codependency. These groups provide a safe space for sharing experiences, receiving support, and learning from others who are on a similar journey.

1. Benefits of Support Groups

SUPPORT GROUPS OFFER numerous benefits for individuals in recovery from codependency. They provide validation, encouragement, and practical strategies for maintaining progress and preventing relapse.

Example: Lisa found that attending a Codependents Anonymous (CoDA) support group provided her with valuable support and insights. The group helped her feel understood and motivated to continue her recovery journey.

Benefits of Support Groups:

- VALIDATION: SHARING experiences with others who understand your struggles provides validation and reduces feelings of isolation.

- Encouragement: Support group members offer encouragement and motivation to stay committed to recovery.

- Practical Strategies: Group members share practical strategies and insights for managing triggers, setting boundaries, and maintaining progress.

- Accountability: Regular attendance and participation in support groups provide accountability and help you stay focused on your recovery goals.

2. Types of Support Groups

VARIOUS TYPES OF SUPPORT groups are available to individuals in recovery from codependency. These groups may be in-person or online, and they may focus on specific aspects of recovery or provide general support.

Example: Mark participated in an online support group for individuals recovering from codependency. The group provided him with a sense of community and support, even though he couldn't attend in-person meetings.

Types of Support Groups:

- CODEPENDENTS ANONYMOUS (CoDA): CoDA is a 12-step support group for individuals recovering from codependency. Meetings are available in-person and online.

- Therapeutic Support Groups: These groups are led by therapists or counselors and provide a structured environment for addressing codependency and related issues.

- Peer-Led Support Groups: These groups are led by individuals who are also in recovery and provide a peer-driven approach to support and accountability.

- Online Support Groups: Online support groups offer flexibility and accessibility for individuals who cannot attend in-person meetings. They provide a platform for sharing experiences and receiving support from others.

3. Building a Supportive Community

BUILDING A SUPPORTIVE community involves creating and nurturing connections with individuals who provide encouragement, validation, and accountability. A supportive community enhances your recovery journey and helps you navigate challenges.

Example: Maria built a supportive community by connecting with friends, family, and support group members who understood her recovery journey. This community provided her with valuable support and encouragement.

Tips for Building a Supportive Community:

- CONNECT WITH LIKE-Minded Individuals: Seek out individuals who share similar experiences and goals. Participate in support groups, workshops, and community events to build connections.

- Nurture Relationships: Nurture relationships with friends, family, and support group members by staying connected and providing mutual support.

- Offer Support: Offer support and encouragement to others in your community. Building reciprocal relationships enhances the sense of connection and mutual support.

- Stay Engaged: Stay engaged with your community by attending meetings, participating in events, and reaching out regularly for support.

4. Participating in Community Activities

PARTICIPATING IN COMMUNITY activities provides opportunities for social connection, personal growth, and enjoyment. Community activities enhance your sense of belonging and contribute to your overall well-being.

Example: Kevin participated in community activities, such as volunteering and attending social events. These activities helped him build new connections and stay engaged with his community.

Benefits of Community Activities:

- SOCIAL CONNECTION: Community activities provide opportunities to connect with others and build meaningful relationships.

- Personal Growth: Engaging in new activities and experiences promotes personal growth and self-discovery.

- Enjoyment and Fulfillment: Participating in activities that bring joy and satisfaction enhances your overall well-being.

- Sense of Belonging: Being part of a community fosters a sense of belonging and reduces feelings of isolation.

Adapting to Life Changes and Challenges

ADAPTING TO LIFE CHANGES and challenges is an important part of long-term recovery. Life is dynamic, and being able to navigate transitions and overcome obstacles is essential for sustaining progress.

1. Developing Resilience

DEVELOPING RESILIENCE involves building the ability to cope with and recover from challenges and setbacks. Resilience helps you stay focused on your recovery goals and navigate life changes effectively.

Example: Lisa developed resilience by practicing mindfulness and self-compassion. These practices helped her stay grounded and cope with challenges more effectively.

Tips for Developing Resilience:

- PRACTICE MINDFULNESS: Mindfulness helps you stay present and aware of your thoughts and emotions, reducing stress and enhancing resilience.

- Cultivate Self-Compassion: Treat yourself with kindness and understanding, especially during difficult times. Recognize that challenges are a natural part of life and recovery.

- Build a Support Network: A strong support network provides encouragement and validation, helping you navigate challenges more effectively.

- Set Realistic Goals: Set realistic goals that are achievable and aligned with your values. Break larger goals into smaller, manageable steps to maintain motivation.

2. Navigating Transitions

NAVIGATING TRANSITIONS, such as changes in relationships, career, or living situations, requires flexibility and adaptability. Being prepared for transitions and having a plan in place can help you manage these changes effectively.

Example: Mark navigated a career transition by seeking support from his therapist and developing a plan for managing the stress and uncertainty. This preparation helped him stay focused on his recovery and adapt to the change.

Steps for Navigating Transitions:

- ANTICIPATE CHANGE: Recognize that transitions are a natural part of life and recovery. Anticipate potential changes and be prepared to adapt.

- Develop a Plan: Create a plan for managing transitions, including specific actions and steps you will take to navigate the change.

- Seek Support: Reach out to your support network for encouragement and guidance during transitions. Share your experiences and seek advice from others who have faced similar changes.

- Stay Flexible: Be open to adjusting your plans and goals as needed. Flexibility helps you adapt to new situations and stay focused on your recovery.

3. Overcoming Obstacles

OVERCOMING OBSTACLES involves addressing challenges and setbacks that may arise during your recovery journey. Developing problem-solving skills and seeking support can help you overcome obstacles effectively.

Example: Maria faced an obstacle when she experienced a relapse in her codependent behaviors. By seeking support from her therapist and support group, she was able to address the setback and develop strategies to prevent future relapse.

Tips for Overcoming Obstacles:

- IDENTIFY THE OBSTACLE: Clearly identify the obstacle or challenge you are facing. Reflect on how it impacts your recovery and well-being.

- Develop a Plan: Create a plan for addressing the obstacle, including specific actions and steps you will take.

- Seek Support: Reach out to your support network for encouragement and guidance. Share your experiences and seek advice from others who have faced similar challenges.

- Practice Self-Compassion: Be kind and compassionate to yourself when faced with obstacles. Recognize that setbacks are a natural part of the recovery process and use them as opportunities to learn and grow.

4. Embracing Change and Growth

EMBRACING CHANGE AND growth involves recognizing that change is a natural part of life and recovery. Being open to new experiences and opportunities for growth enhances your well-being and supports long-term recovery.

Example: Kevin embraced change by seeking new opportunities for personal growth and development. He pursued new hobbies, attended workshops, and sought new experiences that enriched his life and supported his recovery.

Benefits of Embracing Change and Growth:

- PERSONAL DEVELOPMENT: Embracing change provides opportunities for personal growth and self-discovery.

- Enhanced Well-Being: Being open to new experiences and opportunities enhances your overall well-being and satisfaction.

- Increased Resilience: Adapting to change and seeking new opportunities builds resilience and enhances your ability to cope with challenges.

- Sense of Fulfillment: Embracing growth and change contributes to a sense of fulfillment and purpose in life.

5. Staying Focused on Recovery Goals

STAYING FOCUSED ON recovery goals involves regularly reviewing your progress, adjusting your goals as needed, and staying committed to your vision for your recovery and well-being.

Example: Lisa stayed focused on her recovery goals by regularly reviewing her progress and making adjustments as needed. She set new goals and continued to seek support from her therapist and support group.

Tips for Staying Focused on Recovery Goals:

- REGULARLY REVIEW GOALS: Regularly review your recovery goals and assess your progress. Celebrate your achievements and make adjustments as needed.

- Set New Goals: Continuously set new goals that align with your vision for your recovery and well-being. Ensure that your goals are specific, measurable, achievable, relevant, and time-bound (SMART).

- Seek Support: Stay connected with your support network for encouragement and accountability. Share your goals and progress with others who understand your journey.

- Stay Committed: Stay committed to your recovery goals, even during challenging times. Recognize that recovery is an ongoing journey that requires dedication and effort.

Conclusion

Long-term recovery from codependency is an ongoing journey that requires dedication, self-awareness, and continuous effort. Maintaining progress and preventing relapse, engaging in ongoing support groups and communities, and adapting to life changes and challenges are crucial components of this journey. By recognizing and managing triggers, staying committed to self-care, seeking ongoing support, and developing resilience, individuals can sustain their recovery and build a fulfilling, balanced life. Support groups and communities provide validation, encouragement, and practical strategies for maintaining progress, while adapting to life changes and challenges enhances resilience and personal growth. The journey to long-term recovery is challenging, but with dedication, support, and the right strategies, it is possible to overcome codependency and create a life filled with meaningful connections and personal fulfillment.

Chapter 14: Personal Stories of Transformation

Personal stories of transformation can provide powerful inspiration, encouragement, and hope for individuals on their journey to overcoming codependency. In this chapter, we share the stories of several individuals who have successfully navigated the challenges of codependency, highlighting their lessons learned and key takeaways. These stories offer valuable insights and inspiration, encouraging readers to stay committed to their own journeys of recovery and transformation.

Story 1: Jane's Journey to Self-Discovery

BACKGROUND:

Jane, a 35-year-old nurse, had always been the caretaker in her family. Growing up, she felt responsible for her younger siblings and her emotionally volatile mother. As an adult, Jane continued this pattern, constantly putting others' needs before her own. Her low self-esteem and fear of rejection drove her codependent behaviors, leaving her feeling exhausted and unfulfilled.

The Turning Point:

JANE'S TURNING POINT came when she realized she was losing herself in her relationships. Her partner's constant demands and her inability to set boundaries led to burnout. Seeking therapy was a significant step for Jane, as she began to understand the root causes of her codependency.

The Journey:

THROUGH THERAPY, JANE learned to recognize her codependent patterns and the impact of her upbringing on her behavior. She started setting boundaries, saying no to unreasonable requests, and prioritizing her self-care.

Jane joined a support group for codependency, where she connected with others facing similar challenges and received valuable support and encouragement.

Lessons Learned:

- SELF-AWARENESS: UNDERSTANDING the root causes of her codependency was crucial for Jane's recovery. Self-awareness allowed her to recognize and change her patterns.

- Boundaries: Setting and maintaining boundaries was essential for Jane to protect her well-being and reclaim her sense of self.

- Self-Care: Prioritizing self-care helped Jane build resilience and reduce burnout. She learned that taking care of herself was not selfish but necessary.

Key Takeaways:

- RECOGNIZING AND UNDERSTANDING the root causes of codependency is essential for recovery.

- Setting boundaries is crucial for protecting well-being and reclaiming a sense of self.

- Prioritizing self-care is necessary for building resilience and maintaining progress.

Encouragement for Readers:

JANE'S STORY SHOWS that understanding the root causes of codependency, setting boundaries, and prioritizing self-care can lead to significant personal transformation. Readers are encouraged to seek therapy, set boundaries, and prioritize their self-care to overcome codependency and reclaim their sense of self.

Story 2: Mark's Path to Independence

BACKGROUND:

Mark, a 40-year-old marketing executive, struggled with codependency in both his personal and professional relationships. He constantly sought approval from his colleagues and family, fearing rejection and failure. Mark's codependent behaviors included people-pleasing, difficulty setting boundaries, and an overwhelming need for external validation.

The Turning Point:

MARK'S TURNING POINT came when his codependent behaviors began to affect his health. Chronic stress and anxiety led to physical symptoms, prompting Mark to seek help. He began therapy and started to explore the underlying causes of his codependency.

The Journey:

IN THERAPY, MARK LEARNED to identify and challenge his negative thought patterns. He developed healthier coping strategies, such as mindfulness and assertive communication. Mark also joined a support group, where he found validation and support from others on similar journeys. Through these experiences, Mark learned to set boundaries, prioritize his needs, and build his self-esteem.

Lessons Learned:

- MINDFULNESS: PRACTICING mindfulness helped Mark stay present and manage his anxiety. It allowed him to recognize and challenge his negative thought patterns.

- Assertive Communication: Learning to communicate assertively was crucial for Mark to express his needs and set boundaries effectively.

- Self-Esteem: Building self-esteem helped Mark rely less on external validation and more on his sense of self-worth.

Key Takeaways:

- PRACTICING MINDFULNESS can help manage anxiety and challenge negative thought patterns.

- Assertive communication is essential for expressing needs and setting boundaries effectively.

- Building self-esteem reduces reliance on external validation and fosters a stronger sense of self-worth.

Encouragement for Readers:

MARK'S STORY DEMONSTRATES the power of mindfulness, assertive communication, and building self-esteem in overcoming codependency. Readers are encouraged to practice mindfulness, communicate assertively, and work on building their self-esteem to achieve greater independence and self-worth.

Story 3: Maria's Quest for Balance

BACKGROUND:

Maria, a 50-year-old teacher, had always been the caretaker in her relationships. She felt responsible for her partner's and family's happiness, often neglecting her own needs. Maria's codependent behaviors included excessive caretaking, difficulty setting boundaries, and an overwhelming sense of guilt when she tried to prioritize herself.

The Turning Point:

MARIA'S TURNING POINT came when she realized she was neglecting her health and well-being. Chronic fatigue and emotional exhaustion led her to seek therapy. In therapy, Maria began to explore the underlying causes of her codependency and the impact of her upbringing on her behavior.

The Journey:

THROUGH THERAPY, MARIA learned to set boundaries and prioritize her self-care. She joined a support group for codependency, where she found validation and support from others on similar journeys. Maria also began practicing self-compassion and mindfulness, which helped her manage her guilt and anxiety. Over time, Maria developed a healthier balance in her relationships, allowing her to care for herself while still supporting her loved ones.

Lessons Learned:

- BOUNDARIES: SETTING boundaries was crucial for Maria to protect her well-being and reduce her sense of guilt.

- Self-Compassion: Practicing self-compassion helped Maria manage her guilt and anxiety, allowing her to prioritize her self-care.

- Support Groups: Joining a support group provided Maria with validation and encouragement, helping her stay committed to her recovery.

Key Takeaways:

- SETTING BOUNDARIES is essential for protecting well-being and reducing guilt.

- Practicing self-compassion helps manage guilt and anxiety and supports self-care.

- Support groups provide validation and encouragement, enhancing commitment to recovery.

Encouragement for Readers:

MARIA'S STORY HIGHLIGHTS the importance of setting boundaries, practicing self-compassion, and seeking support from others in overcoming codependency. Readers are encouraged to set boundaries, practice self-compassion, and join support groups to achieve a healthier balance in their relationships and prioritize their self-care.

Story 4: Kevin's Journey to Authenticity

BACKGROUND:

Kevin, a 45-year-old architect, struggled with codependency in his personal relationships. He constantly sought approval from his partner and friends, fearing rejection and abandonment. Kevin's codependent behaviors included people-pleasing, difficulty asserting himself, and an overwhelming need for external validation.

The Turning Point:

KEVIN'S TURNING POINT came when his partner ended their relationship, citing Kevin's inability to assert himself and constant need for approval. This experience prompted Kevin to seek therapy and explore the root causes of his codependency.

The Journey:

In therapy, Kevin learned to identify and challenge his negative thought patterns. He developed healthier coping strategies, such as mindfulness and assertive communication. Kevin also joined a support group, where he found validation and support from others on similar journeys. Through these experiences, Kevin learned to assert himself, build his self-esteem, and rely less on external validation.

Lessons Learned:

- ASSERTIVENESS: LEARNING to assert himself was crucial for Kevin to express his needs and build healthier relationships.

- Mindfulness: Practicing mindfulness helped Kevin stay present and manage his anxiety. It allowed him to recognize and challenge his negative thought patterns.

- Self-Esteem: Building self-esteem helped Kevin rely less on external validation and more on his sense of self-worth.

Key Takeaways:

- ASSERTIVENESS IS ESSENTIAL for expressing needs and building healthier relationships.

- Practicing mindfulness can help manage anxiety and challenge negative thought patterns.

- Building self-esteem reduces reliance on external validation and fosters a stronger sense of self-worth.

Encouragement for Readers:

KEVIN'S STORY DEMONSTRATES the power of assertiveness, mindfulness, and building self-esteem in overcoming codependency. Readers are encouraged to practice assertiveness, mindfulness, and work on building their self-esteem to achieve greater authenticity and self-worth.

Story 5: Lisa's Path to Empowerment

BACKGROUND:

Lisa, a 30-year-old social worker, had always been the caretaker in her relationships. She felt responsible for her friends' and family's happiness, often neglecting her own needs. Lisa's codependent behaviors included excessive caretaking, difficulty setting boundaries, and an overwhelming sense of guilt when she tried to prioritize herself.

The Turning Point:

LISA'S TURNING POINT came when she realized she was neglecting her health and well-being. Chronic fatigue and emotional exhaustion led her to seek therapy. In therapy, Lisa began to explore the underlying causes of her codependency and the impact of her upbringing on her behavior.

The Journey:

THROUGH THERAPY, LISA learned to set boundaries and prioritize her self-care. She joined a support group for codependency, where she found validation and support from others on similar journeys. Lisa also began practicing self-compassion and mindfulness, which helped her manage her guilt and anxiety. Over time, Lisa developed a healthier balance in her relationships, allowing her to care for herself while still supporting her loved ones.

Lessons Learned:

- BOUNDARIES: SETTING boundaries was crucial for Lisa to protect her well-being and reduce her sense of guilt.

- Self-Compassion: Practicing self-compassion helped Lisa manage her guilt and anxiety, allowing her to prioritize her self-care.

- Support Groups: Joining a support group provided Lisa with validation and encouragement, helping her stay committed to her recovery.

Key Takeaways:

- SETTING BOUNDARIES is essential for protecting well-being and reducing guilt.

- Practicing self-compassion helps manage guilt and anxiety and supports self-care.

- Support groups provide validation and encouragement, enhancing commitment to recovery.

Encouragement for Readers:

LISA'S STORY HIGHLIGHTS the importance of setting boundaries, practicing self-compassion, and seeking support from others in overcoming codependency. Readers are encouraged to set boundaries, practice self-compassion, and join support groups to achieve a healthier balance in their relationships and prioritize their self-care.

Story 6: John's Journey to Self-Acceptance

Background:

JOHN, A 50-YEAR-OLD accountant, had always struggled with feelings of inadequacy and unworthiness. His low self-esteem drove his codependent behaviors, leading him to constantly seek validation from others. John's codependent behaviors included people-pleasing, difficulty setting boundaries, and an overwhelming need for external approval.

The Turning Point:

JOHN'S TURNING POINT came when his therapist helped him recognize the impact of his upbringing on his codependent behaviors. This insight prompted John to explore his past experiences and develop healthier relationship patterns.

The Journey:

IN THERAPY, JOHN LEARNED to identify and challenge his negative thought patterns. He developed healthier coping strategies, such as mindfulness and self-compassion. John also joined a support group, where he found validation and support from others on similar journeys. Through these experiences, John learned to accept himself, build his self-esteem, and rely less on external validation.

Lessons Learned:

- SELF-ACCEPTANCE: LEARNING to accept himself was crucial for John to build his self-esteem and develop healthier relationship patterns.

- Mindfulness: Practicing mindfulness helped John stay present and manage his anxiety. It allowed him to recognize and challenge his negative thought patterns.

- Support Groups: Joining a support group provided John with validation and encouragement, helping him stay committed to his recovery.

Key Takeaways:

- SELF-ACCEPTANCE IS essential for building self-esteem and developing healthier relationship patterns.

- Practicing mindfulness can help manage anxiety and challenge negative thought patterns.

- Support groups provide validation and encouragement, enhancing commitment to recovery.

Encouragement for Readers:

JOHN'S STORY DEMONSTRATES the power of self-acceptance, mindfulness, and support groups in overcoming codependency. Readers are encouraged to practice self-acceptance, mindfulness, and join support groups to build self-esteem and develop healthier relationship patterns.

Lessons Learned and Key Takeaways

THE PERSONAL STORIES of transformation shared in this chapter highlight several key lessons and takeaways for individuals on their journey to overcoming codependency. These insights can provide valuable guidance and encouragement for readers as they navigate their own recovery journeys.

1. Self-Awareness and Understanding:

Understanding the root causes of codependency and recognizing personal patterns is crucial for recovery. Self-awareness allows individuals to identify and change unhealthy behaviors, paving the way for personal growth and transformation.

2. Boundaries:

Setting and maintaining healthy boundaries is essential for protecting well-being and reclaiming a sense of self. Boundaries help individuals prioritize their needs and reduce the risk of burnout and resentment.

3. Self-Care:

Prioritizing self-care is necessary for building resilience and maintaining progress in recovery. Regular self-care activities promote physical, emotional, and mental well-being, helping individuals sustain their transformation.

4. Mindfulness:

Practicing mindfulness helps individuals stay present and manage anxiety. Mindfulness allows individuals to recognize and challenge negative thought patterns, reducing the impact of triggers and stressors.

5. Assertiveness:

Learning to communicate assertively is crucial for expressing needs and setting boundaries effectively. Assertiveness helps individuals build healthier relationships and reduce reliance on external validation.

6. Self-Compassion:

Practicing self-compassion helps individuals manage guilt and anxiety, supporting self-care and personal growth. Self-compassion fosters a kinder, more accepting relationship with oneself.

7. Support Groups:

Joining support groups provides validation, encouragement, and practical strategies for recovery. Support groups offer a sense of community and accountability, enhancing commitment to long-term recovery.

Encouragement and Hope for Readers

THE PERSONAL STORIES of transformation shared in this chapter offer powerful encouragement and hope for readers on their journey to overcoming codependency. These stories demonstrate that recovery is possible and that individuals can build healthier relationships, develop self-worth, and reclaim their sense of self.

1. Recovery is Possible:

The journeys of Jane, Mark, Maria, Kevin, Lisa, and John show that recovery from codependency is possible with dedication, self-awareness, and support. Each individual faced unique challenges but successfully navigated their paths to transformation.

2. Personal Growth and Transformation:

Personal growth and transformation are achievable through self-awareness, boundary-setting, self-care, mindfulness, assertiveness, self-compassion, and support groups. These practices provide a foundation for lasting change and well-being.

3. You Are Not Alone:

Readers are encouraged to remember that they are not alone in their struggles with codependency. Many individuals have faced similar challenges and found support and encouragement through therapy, support groups, and their communities.

4. Stay Committed:

Recovery is an ongoing journey that requires commitment and effort. Readers are encouraged to stay committed to their recovery goals, seek support when needed, and prioritize their well-being.

5. Embrace Hope:

Hope is a powerful motivator for recovery. Readers are encouraged to embrace hope and believe in their ability to overcome codependency and build a fulfilling, balanced life filled with meaningful connections and personal fulfillment.

Conclusion

Personal stories of transformation offer powerful insights, inspiration, and encouragement for individuals on their journey to overcoming codependency. The journeys of Jane, Mark, Maria, Kevin, Lisa, and John demonstrate that recovery is possible with dedication, self-awareness, and support. By understanding the root causes of codependency, setting boundaries, prioritizing self-care, practicing mindfulness and assertiveness, cultivating self-compassion, and seeking support from others, individuals can achieve personal growth and lasting transformation. Readers are encouraged to stay committed to their recovery, seek support, and embrace hope as they navigate their own paths to a fulfilling, balanced life.

Chapter 15: Moving Forward

Moving forward from codependency towards a healthy and fulfilling life requires setting goals, continuing personal growth, and building balanced relationships. This chapter provides comprehensive guidance on setting goals for a healthy future, fostering ongoing personal growth and self-improvement, and creating a life filled with balanced, fulfilling relationships.

Setting Goals for a Healthy Future

SETTING GOALS IS ESSENTIAL for maintaining direction and motivation as you move forward from codependency. Clear, achievable goals provide a roadmap for personal growth and relationship improvement.

1. Understanding the Importance of Goal Setting

GOAL SETTING HELPS individuals clarify their vision for the future, prioritize their efforts, and stay focused on their recovery journey. Well-defined goals provide a sense of purpose and direction, making it easier to stay committed to personal growth and healthy relationship patterns.

Example: Jane set specific goals for her recovery, such as developing healthier boundaries, improving her self-esteem, and building a support network. These goals helped her stay focused and motivated as she navigated her recovery journey.

Benefits of Goal Setting:

- PROVIDES CLARITY AND direction for personal growth and recovery.

- Enhances motivation and commitment to achieving desired outcomes.

- Helps prioritize efforts and allocate resources effectively.

- Facilitates tracking progress and celebrating achievements.

2. Setting SMART Goals

SMART GOALS ARE SPECIFIC, measurable, achievable, relevant, and time-bound. This framework helps ensure that goals are clear, realistic, and aligned with your values and priorities.

Example: Mark set a SMART goal to improve his self-esteem by practicing positive affirmations daily and attending a self-esteem workshop within the next three months. This goal was specific, measurable, achievable, relevant, and time-bound, providing a clear path for progress.

Steps to Set SMART Goals:

- SPECIFIC: CLEARLY define the goal, specifying what you want to achieve.

- Measurable: Determine how you will measure progress and success.

- Achievable: Ensure the goal is realistic and attainable within your resources and constraints.

- Relevant: Align the goal with your values, priorities, and long-term vision.

- Time-Bound: Set a deadline for achieving the goal, creating a sense of urgency and focus.

3. Identifying Personal Values and Priorities

IDENTIFYING PERSONAL values and priorities helps ensure that your goals are meaningful and aligned with what matters most to you. Reflecting on your values and priorities can provide clarity and direction as you set goals for a healthy future.

Example: Maria identified her personal values of self-care, healthy relationships, and personal growth. These values guided her goal-setting process, ensuring that her goals were aligned with what mattered most to her.

Steps to Identify Personal Values and Priorities:

- REFLECT ON YOUR VALUES: Consider what is most important to you in life, such as health, relationships, personal growth, and fulfillment.

- Identify Priorities: Determine your top priorities based on your values and current life circumstances.

- Align Goals with Values: Ensure that your goals are aligned with your values and priorities, enhancing their relevance and meaningfulness.

- Review Regularly: Regularly review your values and priorities to ensure they continue to align with your goals and desired outcomes.

4. Creating a Goal-Setting Plan

CREATING A GOAL-SETTING plan involves outlining the steps you will take to achieve your goals, identifying potential challenges, and establishing a timeline for progress. A well-structured plan provides a clear roadmap for success.

Example: Kevin created a goal-setting plan to improve his communication skills. He outlined steps such as enrolling in a communication workshop, practicing active listening, and seeking feedback from friends. He also identified potential challenges and set a timeline for achieving his goals.

Steps to Create a Goal-Setting Plan:

- DEFINE THE GOAL: CLEARLY define the goal and its desired outcome.

- Outline Steps: Break down the goal into actionable steps and tasks.

- Identify Challenges: Consider potential obstacles and challenges and develop strategies to address them.

- Set a Timeline: Establish a timeline for achieving the goal, including milestones and deadlines.

- Track Progress: Regularly track your progress and make adjustments as needed.

5. Reviewing and Adjusting Goals

REGULARLY REVIEWING and adjusting goals is essential for maintaining progress and adapting to changing circumstances. This process helps ensure that your goals remain relevant and achievable as you move forward.

Example: Lisa regularly reviewed her goals and progress with her therapist. She made adjustments as needed to address new challenges and opportunities, ensuring that her goals remained aligned with her evolving needs and priorities.

Steps to Review and Adjust Goals:

- SCHEDULE REGULAR REVIEWS: Set aside time regularly to review your goals and progress.

- Reflect on Progress: Reflect on your achievements and challenges, considering what has worked well and what needs adjustment.

- Make Adjustments: Adjust your goals, steps, and timeline as needed to address new challenges and opportunities.

- Celebrate Successes: Celebrate your achievements and progress, reinforcing your commitment to your goals.

Continuing Personal Growth and Self-Improvement

CONTINUING PERSONAL growth and self-improvement is essential for maintaining progress and achieving long-term success in overcoming codependency. This process involves ongoing self-reflection, learning, and development.

1. Embracing Lifelong Learning

LIFELONG LEARNING INVOLVES continuously seeking opportunities to learn and grow, both personally and professionally. Embracing lifelong learning fosters personal development, resilience, and adaptability.

Example: Jane embraced lifelong learning by enrolling in courses, attending workshops, and reading books on personal development and healthy relationships. These activities helped her stay engaged and motivated in her recovery journey.

Ways to Embrace Lifelong Learning:

- ENROLL IN COURSES: Take courses and workshops on topics related to personal development, relationships, and self-care.

- Read Books: Read books and articles on personal growth, self-improvement, and mental health.

- Attend Seminars: Attend seminars and conferences to gain new insights and connect with others on similar journeys.

- Seek Feedback: Seek feedback from trusted friends, family, and professionals to identify areas for improvement and growth.

2. Practicing Self-Reflection

SELF-REFLECTION INVOLVES regularly examining your thoughts, feelings, and behaviors to gain insights and identify areas for growth. Practicing self-reflection enhances self-awareness and fosters personal development.

Example: Mark practiced self-reflection by journaling daily and reflecting on his experiences and progress. This practice helped him gain insights into his behaviors and identify areas for improvement.

Tips for Practicing Self-Reflection:

- JOURNAL REGULARLY: Keep a journal to record your thoughts, feelings, and experiences. Reflect on your entries to gain insights and identify patterns.

- Set Aside Quiet Time: Set aside regular quiet time for self-reflection, free from distractions and interruptions.

- Ask Reflective Questions: Ask yourself reflective questions, such as "What did I learn today?" and "How can I improve?"

- Seek Feedback: Seek feedback from trusted friends, family, and professionals to gain different perspectives and insights.

3. Cultivating Positive Habits

CULTIVATING POSITIVE habits involves developing routines and behaviors that support your well-being and personal growth. Positive habits enhance your physical, emotional, and mental health, contributing to long-term success.

Example: Maria cultivated positive habits such as regular exercise, mindfulness meditation, and healthy eating. These habits supported her well-being and helped her stay focused on her recovery goals.

Steps to Cultivate Positive Habits:

- IDENTIFY DESIRED HABITS: Identify the habits you want to develop based on your values and goals.

- Start Small: Start with small, manageable changes to build momentum and confidence.

- Create a Routine: Establish a routine that incorporates your desired habits into your daily life.

- Track Progress: Track your progress and celebrate your achievements to reinforce positive behaviors.

- Stay Consistent: Stay consistent in practicing your habits, even during challenging times.

4. Seeking Ongoing Support

SEEKING ONGOING SUPPORT is crucial for maintaining personal growth and self-improvement. Support from friends, family, therapists, and support groups provides encouragement, validation, and accountability.

Example: Kevin continued to attend therapy sessions and support group meetings regularly. This ongoing support helped him stay committed to his personal growth and navigate challenges effectively.

Tips for Seeking Ongoing Support:

- STAY CONNECTED: STAY connected with your support network, including friends, family, therapists, and support groups.

- Participate in Support Groups: Attend support group meetings regularly to connect with others and receive mutual support.

- Seek Professional Help: Continue to work with a therapist or counselor to address any ongoing challenges and receive guidance and support.

- Build a Diverse Support Network: Build a diverse support network that includes different types of support, such as emotional, practical, and social.

5. Embracing Change and Growth

EMBRACING CHANGE AND growth involves recognizing that change is a natural part of life and recovery. Being open to new experiences and opportunities for growth enhances your well-being and supports long-term success.

Example: Lisa embraced change by seeking new opportunities for personal growth and development. She pursued new hobbies, attended workshops, and sought new experiences that enriched her life and supported her recovery.

Benefits of Embracing Change and Growth:

- PERSONAL DEVELOPMENT: Embracing change provides opportunities for personal growth and self-discovery.

- Enhanced Well-Being: Being open to new experiences and opportunities enhances your overall well-being and satisfaction.

- Increased Resilience: Adapting to change and seeking new opportunities builds resilience and enhances your ability to cope with challenges.

- Sense of Fulfillment: Embracing growth and change contributes to a sense of fulfillment and purpose in life.

Building a Life of Balanced, Fulfilling Relationships

BUILDING A LIFE OF balanced, fulfilling relationships is essential for long-term success in overcoming codependency. This process involves developing healthy relationship patterns, fostering mutual respect and trust, and creating a supportive and nurturing environment.

1. Developing Healthy Relationship Patterns**

DEVELOPING HEALTHY relationship patterns involves recognizing and changing codependent behaviors, setting boundaries, and fostering mutual respect and trust. Healthy relationship patterns enhance your well-being and contribute to fulfilling connections.

Example: Jane developed healthy relationship patterns by setting boundaries, practicing assertive communication, and fostering mutual respect and trust in her relationships. These changes led to more balanced and fulfilling connections.

Steps to Develop Healthy Relationship Patterns:

- RECOGNIZE CODEPENDENT Behaviors: Identify and challenge codependent behaviors, such as people-pleasing and excessive caretaking.

- Set Boundaries: Set and maintain healthy boundaries to protect your well-being and foster mutual respect.

- Practice Assertive Communication: Communicate your needs and feelings assertively, while also respecting the needs and feelings of others.

- Foster Mutual Respect and Trust: Build relationships based on mutual respect and trust, where both partners feel valued and supported.

- Seek Healthy Role Models: Seek out healthy role models who demonstrate balanced, fulfilling relationships and learn from their behaviors and practices.

2. Fostering Mutual Respect and Trust

MUTUAL RESPECT AND trust are foundational to healthy, balanced relationships. Fostering mutual respect and trust involves valuing each other's perspectives, honoring commitments, and maintaining open and honest communication.

Example: Mark fostered mutual respect and trust in his relationships by valuing his partner's perspectives, honoring his commitments, and maintaining open and honest communication. These practices strengthened his relationships and enhanced his well-being.

Tips for Fostering Mutual Respect and Trust:

- VALUE EACH OTHER'S Perspectives: Recognize and appreciate the unique perspectives and experiences of your partner.

- Honor Commitments: Follow through on your commitments and promises, demonstrating reliability and trustworthiness.

- Maintain Open Communication: Communicate openly and honestly about your thoughts, feelings, and needs.

- Show Appreciation: Express appreciation and gratitude for your partner's contributions and efforts.

- Build a Foundation of Trust: Build trust through consistent and honest behavior, creating a secure and supportive relationship.

3. Creating a Supportive and Nurturing Environment

CREATING A SUPPORTIVE and nurturing environment involves fostering a sense of safety, understanding, and encouragement in your relationships. A supportive environment enhances emotional well-being and contributes to fulfilling connections.

Example: Maria created a supportive and nurturing environment in her relationships by offering empathy, understanding, and encouragement. This environment fostered emotional well-being and strengthened her connections with loved ones.

Steps to Create a Supportive and Nurturing Environment:

- OFFER EMPATHY AND Understanding: Practice empathy and understanding by listening to your partner's feelings and experiences without judgment.

- Provide Encouragement: Offer encouragement and support for your partner's goals and aspirations.

- Foster Emotional Safety: Create an environment where both partners feel safe to express their thoughts and feelings without fear of judgment or rejection.

- Celebrate Achievements: Celebrate each other's achievements and milestones, reinforcing positive behaviors and contributions.

- Nurture Each Other's Well-Being: Prioritize each other's well-being and support each other in self-care and personal growth.

4. Building a Diverse Support Network

BUILDING A DIVERSE support network involves connecting with individuals who provide different types of support, such as emotional, practical, and social. A diverse support network enhances your well-being and contributes to fulfilling relationships.

Example: Kevin built a diverse support network that included friends, family, support group members, and professional mentors. This network provided him with a wide range of support and encouragement, enhancing his well-being and relationships.

Tips for Building a Diverse Support Network:

- CONNECT WITH FRIENDS and Family: Build and maintain relationships with friends and family who provide emotional support and understanding.

- Join Support Groups: Participate in support groups to connect with others who share similar experiences and provide mutual support.

- Seek Professional Mentors: Seek out professional mentors who can offer guidance and support for your personal and professional growth.

- Engage in Community Activities: Participate in community activities and events to build new connections and expand your support network.

- Maintain Reciprocal Relationships: Build reciprocal relationships where both partners provide and receive support and encouragement.

5. Practicing Self-Compassion and Compassion for Others

PRACTICING SELF-COMPASSION and compassion for others enhances your well-being and fosters healthier, more fulfilling relationships. Self-compassion involves treating yourself with kindness and understanding, while compassion for others involves offering empathy and support.

Example: Lisa practiced self-compassion by treating herself with kindness and understanding during challenging times. She also practiced compassion for others by offering empathy and support to her friends and family. These practices enhanced her well-being and relationships.

Benefits of Practicing Self-Compassion and Compassion for Others:

- ENHANCED WELL-BEING: Self-compassion and compassion for others enhance emotional well-being and reduce stress.

- Stronger Relationships: Compassionate behaviors foster trust, understanding, and connection in relationships.

- Greater Resilience: Self-compassion builds resilience and helps individuals cope with challenges more effectively.

- Increased Empathy: Compassion for others enhances empathy and understanding, creating more supportive and nurturing relationships.

Tips for Practicing Self-Compassion and Compassion for Others:

- BE KIND TO YOURSELF: Treat yourself with the same kindness and understanding you would offer a friend. Recognize that challenges and setbacks are a natural part of life and recovery.

- Practice Mindfulness: Practice mindfulness to stay present and aware of your thoughts and feelings. Mindfulness enhances self-compassion and reduces stress.

- Offer Empathy: Practice empathy by listening to others' feelings and experiences without judgment. Offer support and understanding to those in need.

- Engage in Acts of Kindness: Engage in acts of kindness and support for others, such as offering a listening ear, providing practical assistance, or expressing appreciation.

- Reflect on Compassion: Reflect on the importance of compassion in your life and relationships. Consider how practicing compassion enhances your well-being and connections with others.

Conclusion

Moving forward from codependency towards a healthy and fulfilling life involves setting goals, continuing personal growth, and building balanced relationships. By setting SMART goals, embracing lifelong learning, practicing self-reflection, cultivating positive habits, and seeking ongoing support, individuals can achieve lasting transformation and personal growth. Developing healthy relationship patterns, fostering mutual respect and trust, creating a supportive and nurturing environment, building a diverse support network, and practicing self-compassion and compassion for others are essential for building a life filled with balanced, fulfilling relationships. The journey to overcoming codependency is challenging, but with dedication, support, and the right strategies, it is possible to create a fulfilling, balanced life filled with meaningful connections and personal fulfillment. Readers are encouraged to stay committed to their recovery, set goals, embrace personal growth, and build healthy relationships as they move forward towards a brighter future.

Don't miss out!

Visit the website below and you can sign up to receive emails whenever Timothy Scott Phillips publishes a new book. There's no charge and no obligation.

https://books2read.com/r/B-A-KCQWC-ORTJF

BOOKS 2 READ

Connecting independent readers to independent writers.

About the Author

Timothy Scott Phillips is a dedicated author specializing in non-fiction self-help books that empower readers to overcome challenges and embrace personal growth. With a passion for mental health, resilience, and self-improvement, Timothy combines research-based insights with practical strategies to inspire lasting change. His work reflects a deep commitment to helping individuals navigate life's complexities, build confidence, and unlock their full potential. When he's not writing, Timothy enjoys mentoring, exploring nature, and connecting with his readers to share stories of transformation and hope. His books are a testament to the power of perseverance and the human spirit.